CRANKING

UP

STEVIE
WONDER

**Concise, fun, high-energy tours through
the catalogs of major musical acts, in just 11 songs**

Series Editor: Arthur Lizie

Other titles in Backbeat's GOES TO 11 series:

Cranking Up Rush: Their Musical Legacy in 11 Songs
by Adrien Begrand

Cranking Up Taylor Swift: Her Musical Career in 11 Songs
by Phoebe E. Hughes

CRANKING

UP

STEVIE
WONDER

HIS MUSICAL LEGACY IN
11 SONGS

ARTHUR LIZIE

Backbeat
Books

Bloomsbury Publishing Group, Inc.
Backbeatbooks.com

Distributed by NATIONAL BOOK NETWORK

British Library Cataloguing in Publication Information available

Library of Congress Cataloging-in-Publication Data

Names: Lizie, Arthur E., author.
Title: Cranking up Stevie Wonder: his musical legacy in 11 songs / Arthur
   Lizie.
Description: Essex, Connecticut: Backbeat, 2024. | Series: Goes to 11 ;
   no. 1
Identifiers: LCCN 2024023522 | ISBN 9781493072095 (paperback) | ISBN
   9781493072101 (ebook)
Subjects: LCSH: Wonder, Stevie Criticism and interpretation. | Popular
   music--History and criticism. | Rhythm and blues music—History and
   criticism. | Soul music—History and criticism.
Classification: LCC ML410.W836 L58 2024 | DDC
   782.421644092—dc23/eng/20240522
LC record available at https://lccn.loc.gov/2024023522

CONTENTS

INTRODUCTION

Sometime in the early 2000s, storytelling began to both expand and fracture. Once, a single feature-length film captured society's collective imagination. Then, almost overnight, a similar story was told in kaleidoscopic fashion in ten episodes over ten hours. Three hours with Don Michael Corleone became eight hours and then six seasons with Tony Soprano. A singular Tom Hanks in *Cast Away* became the multicharacter epic *Lost*. The narrative arc changed, becoming longer, more diffuse, and much deeper at individual plot points.

This brings us to our subject at hand: Stevie Wonder. The Stevie Wonder Story has been told many times in a number of similar feature-film ways. It's a narrative arc we understand in general and are intrigued by in particular. He wasn't born in Little Rock or "hard time" Mississippi, but he had a tough early life, turned his prodigious musical skills into a recording contract at the age of eleven, and found early Motown success. He then fought to establish himself on his own terms, achieved worldwide acclaim, and finally settled into a mostly content life, with occasional narrative disruptions. It's the Horatio Alger myth. It's a story we like to tell ourselves.

But the story we're telling here isn't exactly this "Stevie Wonder Story." While we are traveling more or less chronologically through the life of Stevland Hardaway Morris, né Judkins, we're going deeper at a few individual plot points rather than strictly following the feature-length version: eleven songs from different places in the narrative arc. The hope is that a closer look at these discrete points, with some backstory for each song and an exploration of the musical and cultural environment into which the song was released, will give a fuller understanding of what Stevie Wonder means in popular music culture and how he got to that point. Ultimately, he's not Tom Hanks stranded on an island with a volleyball, but he's an artist among other artists, a human in the world, continually pulling in and spreading out songs and ideas and culture: Stevie as musical vortex.

The first three chapters cover Wonder's first decade at Motown. Stevie finds almost immediate commercial acclaim (chapter 1: "Fingertips—Part 2") and then meets with varied success as Motown can't quite find a genre or marketing fit (chapter 2: "Alfie"). But there's one genre Stevie does master, and that's Motown's distinctive brand of R&B/soul/pop (chapter 3: "Uptight [Everything's Alright]").

The next three chapters tackle Wonder's wildly creative independent period from 1971 to 1976, when Stevie had a lot to say and said it in an innovative and unique voice. Chapter 4 ("Do Yourself a Favor") explores Stevie's transition from R&B star to funkmeister, with a deeper look at technologies and fellow travelers who spurred his musical growth. Admiring that Stevie crossed musical boundaries, chapter 5 ("Superstition") looks at his relationship with rock music and musicians, especially the Rolling Stones and the Beatles. Chapter 6 ("Boogie on Reggae Woman") explores what might be Stevie's most perfect song and his signature go-to instrument, the harmonica.

The second half of the book covers the 1980s and beyond. Chapter 7 ("Happy Birthday") explores Wonder's undying dedication to social activism and social justice. Chapter 8 ("I Just Called to Say I Love You") gets into the artist's midcareer missteps—where's Stevie's line between easy to listen to and easy listening? Chapter 9 ("Fun Day") recounts his soundtrack work, while chapter 10 ("So What the Fuss") digs into his collaborations. Finally, chapter 11 ("Sir Duke") explores Stevie's live musical legacy.

And cranked to eleven, you have a new Stevie Wonder Story.

1

"FINGERTIPS—PART 2"

Novelty Act

The top of the US singles chart has been scaled by all manner of curiosities. We've had shrill serenades like "Tiptoe through the Tulips" (a 1968 top 20 hit for Tiny Tim, but a 1929 number one for Nick Lucas, the "Crooning Troubadour"), silly songs like "Disco Duck" by Rick Dees and His Cast of Idiots, and synergistic successes like "Maniac," the *Flashdance*-fueled hit by Wonderlove guitarist Michael Sembello. We've had short songs like "Old Town Road," by Lil Nas X featuring Billy Ray Cyrus, which spent more days at the top of the charts, 133, than it was seconds long, 113. And we've had Stevie Wonder.

Twenty-first-century Stevie Wonder is a musical legend, with ten number-one pop and twenty number-one R&B hits, but he began as a curiosity—a blind, Black, eleven-year-old with a freaky talent for bongos, drums, and harmonica. He first hit number one in 1963 as Little Stevie Wonder with "Fingerprints—Part 2." The harmonica rave is a novelty song from a novelty act, and beyond that, unusual at the top of the single charts as both a live performance and a B-side. It's also a semi-instrumental, which is a bit like being semi-pregnant.

THE BACKSTORY

In 1960, Wonder (then Judkins) formed a musical duo with his friend John Glover, Steven and John. Glover's cousin was Ronnie White of the Miracles. The Miracles were the first group to release a Motown LP, *Hi . . . We're the Miracles*, on the Tamla imprint. Why call it Tamla? Greek goddess of rhythm and blues? Nope. Motown owner Berry Gordy wanted to name his label "Tammy" because he loved Debbie Reynolds's 1957 number-one pop hit, but Tammy was already copyrighted. Tamla—less elegant but more memorable.

Miracles singer/songwriter White got the boys an audition at Hitsville U.S.A. on September 23, 1961. Gordy's right-hand man Mickey Stevenson was surprised to discover that Wonder was blind and was worried he'd trip over things in the studio. He needn't have worried—Stevie deftly navigated the studio, and Steven and John nailed the audition. Gordy decided to sign the duo on the spot. The spot was delayed because of legal issues surrounding their ages—Judkins was eleven years old—and partly because Gordy was impressed with Stevie's musical talent but didn't like his voice.

Once signed, there was confusion about how to cultivate and market Judkins. These "direction" problems persisted until Stevie Wonder took control of his destiny in 1971. The confusion shows up his 1962 debut release, "I Call It Pretty Music, but the Old People Call It the Blues." The two-part single features an upbeat, almost poppy vocal on the A-side but a slow, almost bluesy instrumental on the superior B-side. Which is the real Stevie?

But there was good news: the A-side went to 101 on the pop charts! So how do you capitalize on this minor success? With the September 1962 instrumental LP *The Jazz Soul of Little Stevie*, of course. But the LP didn't include the "hit" single or, for that matter, any single. And then it was followed by a non-LP single, "Little Water Boy," a supper-club rave-up duet credited to man-about-Motown Clarence Paul, with second billing going to "Little Stevie Wonder on drums and vocals." The song is a bizarre tale in which the elder Paul tries to convince the youngster to get off his ass and fetch some water for a mere forty cents, an unintentional metaphor for Motown labor habits. Faithful employee Stevie capitulated and fetched the water. Both the LP and the single bombed.

But they tried it again. A month later. Gordy figured, Stevie's Black and blind—he's the new Ray Charles! October 1962's *Tribute to Uncle Ray* matched the debut LP's lack of success, but this time with vocals.

December 1962 saw another attempt at a single breakthrough, "Contract on Love." It went nowhere, buried in part by the ridiculous quality of product erupting from Hitsville at the time. Stevie's single was Tamla 54074. Tamla 54073 was the Miracles' "You Really Got a Hold on Me," and Tamla 54075 was Marvin Gaye's "Hitch Hike." Easy to get lost in that company.

But Stevie didn't get lost on his way to the stage. He was part of Motown's inaugural Motortown Revue package tour, which started on October 26 with a seven-night stay at Washington's Howard Theatre and ran through mid-December 1962. Newly signed and without a hit, Stevie billed low, typically performing either his debut single or "Don't You Know" from the Ray Charles album. But the crowd loved him, and Stevie loved the stage and didn't want to leave, so much so that Paul's yanking him off the stage by necessity became part of the act.

THE SONG

After Stevie's success onstage and failure on vinyl, Gordy decided to go to the tapes for a solution. At the Motortown Revue dry run, he had recorded a seven-song June 1962 performance at Chicago's Regal Theater, the Bronzeville venue every Black performer who was anybody had played since its 1928 opening. The show was good enough to release.

Stevie Wonder's *Recorded Live: The 12 Year Old Genius* saw daylight in May 1963. The month also saw the release of the most important live album in soul music history, James Brown's *Live at the Apollo*. Stevie's now curio LP made number one on the pop charts, the first Motown LP to do so; James's forever-masterpiece stalled at number two.

The first side of *Recorded Live* includes the "Little Water Boy" B-side, "La La La La La," and two tracks from the first album: the

Marvin Gaye/Clarence Paul track "Soul Bongo," and "Fingertips." Side two offers four songs made famous by Ray Charles.

On the studio album, "Fingertips" is a pleasant but unremarkable three-minute flute-based jazz instrumental. On the live album, it expands into a six-minute, forty-second, full-soul energy assault as Stevie soaks up the audience's love and sends it back twice over. It's a celebration of life.

The only single from the album was released May 21, 1963. The LP version was edited to a part 1 and part 2, both clocking in at 2:49. The first side starts slowly and builds, but the second side keeps the foot on the pedal the whole way. It starts with a Stevie shout-out: "Everybody say yeah!" The band, with Marvin Gaye on drums, grooves, and Stevie raps. He picks up the harmonica and jams, getting big laughs with a "Mary Had a Little Lamb" riff. At 2:06, Stevie leaves the stage as the band heads into their act-transition vamp. Dead silence at 2:16. But the harmonica starts up again, and then someone shouts, "What key?" The band picks up, and Stevie jams some more. There's no cape, but we enjoy the same soul resurrection that James Brown perfected and shared on *Live at the Apollo*'s "Please Please Please" medley.

A star is born.

BLIND TOM

Music historian James E. Perone parallels Wonder's early novelty-act status with the promotion of nineteenth-century performer

Thomas Wiggins/Bethune. As boys, both were promoted as blind, Black musical prodigies and paraded around the country.

In 1857 at the age of eight, the slave Wiggins was brought on tour as Blind Tom by his master, James N. Bethune. According to researcher Barbara Schmidt, Blind Tom was a musical "autistic savant," able to mimic and create sounds on the piano to the point that a teacher claimed his "musical abilities were beyond comprehension." He played a command performance for President James Buchanan, and media reports compared him to Mozart. Mark Twain was a fan.

Near the end of the Civil War, promoter Tabbs Gross, known as the "Black P. T. Barnum," had a claim on Blind Tom, but lost in court to Bethune. Even after the end of slavery, Blind Tom was never legitimately set free. Into the 1870s, Bethune continued to make about $300,000 a year from Tom in 2020 dollars.

Wiggins wrote, adapted, and performed hundreds of tunes. What remains and is performed today are primarily crisp piano pieces, such as "The Battle of Manassas" and "March Timpani." To contemporary ears, much of this material sounds like silent movie music intended to accompany scenes of the old South.

For historian Perone, the distinction between Wonder and Wiggins is that the latter was never able to throw off the novelty status and grow as an artist. Without pushing the point too hard, Blind Tom, given his performing name by Bethune, was not able to do this due to his status in the late-1800s United States as an autistic enslaved man, freed but attached to a dishonest owner. Stevie, given the name Wonder by Berry Gordy, was only able to achieve his full potential once he reached maturity and (mostly) broke free of the indentured terms of his childhood Motown contract.

The Ed Sullivan Show

It took a year, but Gordy was able to land Wonder on *The Ed Sullivan Show* on May 3, 1964. It was a few weeks before the release of a new single, "Hey Harmonica Man," which would be his second pop top 30 hit, but Stevie still performed "Fingertips."

Stevie is all arms and sunglasses and harmonica, alone and owning the stage. As on the live single, he feeds off the energy of the crowd. It's a successful appearance, although Sullivan doesn't seem overly pleased. This may explain why even though he supported Black performers, and especially Motown acts—the Supremes appeared fourteen times—Sullivan featured Stevie only one more time, December 15, 1968, to perform brief versions of "For Once in My Life" and "You Met Your Match."

Stunningly, Stevie's appearance on that 1964 Sullivan show isn't the closest link in the broadcast between Blind Tom's time and a pre–Civil Rights Act America. That would be *America, Be Seated!*

Stumbling upon the Sullivan footage of *America, Be Seated!* context-free, the three-and-a-half-minute excerpt is cringeworthy in its stereotypical race and gender assumptions. Dressed for a day out on the town, Mae Barnes, who popularized the Charleston on Broadway in the 1920s, and a young Lola Falana vamp it up on

"That's How a Woman Gets Her Man." This is met in retort by a young, dandified Louis Gossett Jr. with "Don't Let a Woman Get You, Man." It's like watching a sketch-comedy parody of a minstrel show, but without the parody. Although it was a parody. Just not, apparently, as presented on the Sullivan show.

America, Be Seated! was Louisiana's theatrical contribution to the 1964 New York World's Fair. Landing somewhere between vaudeville and a minstrel show, the production was a satire of stereotypical racial values and was endorsed by the NAACP. The show barely moved from Flushing Meadows to Broadway before closing. America was ready for cute blind Black boys, but not so much for a satire of the culture from which cute blind Black boys emerged.

Make It Sound the Same, Only Different

Every number-one song is a novelty song. In 2017, business professors Noah Askin and Michael Mauskapf looked at sixty years of US number-one songs for "product features and optimal differentiation." What they found was that hit songs "sound similar to whatever else is popular at the time, but also have enough of a unique sound to help them stand out as distinctive." In Hollywood, this is known as "make it the same, only different."

Askin and Mauskapf used a computer algorithm to analyze number-one songs along eight dimensions: Danceability, tempo, energy, acousticness, liveness, speechiness, instrumentalness, and valence. The first seven are somewhat self-explanatory, but the final one's a head-scratcher. Valence analyzes a song's "positiveness"—a feeling that is aligned but doesn't quite measure up with major or minor keys. For example, "I Want to Hold Your Hand" and Stevie's "Part-Time Lover" both hit it out of the valence park.

An interactive website hosted by the Columbia Business School offers a visual dimensional analysis of each number-one song, with the ability to compare songs to the average hit from the previous year and any hit from the same year. It also lists the most similar and dissimilar number-one hits. What do we learn about "Fingertips?"

In comparison with the average hit of 1962, Wonder's was bolder in terms of tempo, energy, speechiness, and liveness, was slightly more instrumental, but lags in the other three categories. That makes sense considering that the Four Seasons' "Big Girls Don't Cry" and "Sherry" spent about 20 percent of 1962 at the top of the charts. Both those songs were singable and extremely high on valence, although valence here might be a code word for ear-piercing.

"Fingertips" surpassed all other top hits of the year on energy, which is the song's main attribute. For algorithm-similar songs, only the Beach Boys' "I Get Around" and Roy Orbison's "Oh, Pretty Woman" have more oomph. It also scored remarkably high on liveness, although not as high as one might expect from a "live" song. For 1963, it was surpassed in liveness by the Angels' "My Boy-friend's Back," a barely produced demo. The "similar song" over the six decades with the highest liveness quality is Frankie Valli's "My Eyes Adored You" from 1974. Valli's two 1962 Four Seasons hits were exceptionally low on liveness, but this tune from nonmajor Private Stock Records didn't bust the budget on fancy-pants studio production. Another similar tune is the bombastic "Hello, Dolly" by Louis "Satchmo" Armstrong, later name-checked in "Sir Duke."

Among the most dissimilar songs are *Billboard*'s most popular song of 1962, Acker Bilk's continuously forgettable clarinet instrumental "Stranger on the Shore," and the Silver Convention's 1975 disco hit, "Fly, Robin Fly."

Hit Live and B-Sides

Pop music live LPs have typically been commerce first and art second, money-generating placeholders featuring rerecordings of familiar tunes to fill the gap between new studio releases. Rare have been the live albums that have featured all new material, such as the MC5's *Kick Out the Jams* and Neil Young and Crazy Horse's *Rust Never Sleeps* (sort of). And often, as with many James Brown discs (although pointedly not *Live at the Apollo*), live albums weren't even live albums, just repackaged studio tracks with added crowd noise.

Although captured at a live performance, *Recorded Live: The 12 Year Old Genius* fits the placeholder bill. It has no new songs, although calling any of the seven tunes familiar is a stretch, unless one considers the four Ray Charles songs. It arrived in May 1963, a full seven months after the previous studio LP and seven months before the December 1963 release of *With a Song in My Heart*. Certainly stopgap.

It is somewhat unusual that "Fingertips" was culled from the LP as a single. As a quick cash-in, live albums aren't always promoted with singles. Raise your hand if you remember that the Rolling Stones released Chuck Berry's "Little Queenie" as a 1971 single from *Get Yer Ya-Ya's Out!* Raise both hands if you remember that it went top five in Switzerland. Raise another hand if you put any stock in Swiss charts: to give some perspective, the follow-up at the top of the Swiss charts to Stevie's "I Just Called to Say I Love You" was a six-week run by "When the Rain Begins to Fall" by Jermaine Jackson and Pia Zadora. Jermaine Jackson and Pia Zadora. Six weeks. Let that sink in.

It was even more unusual that the live "Fingertips" single went to number one, as only a handful of live songs have hit the top of the charts. The other live rock-era novelty song to hit number one is Berry's 1972 "My Ding-a-Ling." The song was written and recorded by Dave Bartholomew in 1952. Bartholomew would hit number one in 1955 as cowriter of the Fats Domino classic "Ain't That a Shame." Berry recorded the masturbation celebration at the Lanchester Arts Festival in Coventry, England, on February 3, 1972, a bill he shared with Pink Floyd. Fingertips and my ding-a-ling—makes sense.

Two live number-one live recordings were rerecordings of hits that failed to reach the summit. "Mony Mony" was a number-three hit for Tommy James and the Shondells in 1968. Billy Idol's studio take on the song stalled short of the top 100 in 1981, but his 1987 live version from the hits LP *Vital Idol* hit number one. And it's horrible. The cheesy synth fills accompanied by tuneless barking make it sound like the baseball ballpark organist was joined during the seventh-inning stretch by a slightly inebriated beer vendor.

Knight Bachelor Elton John hit number two in 1974 with "Don't Let the Sun Go Down on Me," then hit number one with a live duet version with George Michael in November 1991. It's superior to Idol's live "Mony Mony," and we'll leave it at that.

This brings us to another Knight Bachelor and Stevie number-one collaborator, Sir Paul McCartney. McCartney and Wings hit the top of the charts in April 1980 with "Coming Up (Live at Glasgow)," the B-side of the studio version of the song. The studio version comes from *McCartney II*, an electronically experimental album that gave Columbia Records doubts about its commercial viability. To soften the blow, the label planted the more traditional rock live version on the B-side, then pushed it for radio and included it as a bonus one-sided 7-inch with the McCartney solo LP. Mission accomplished—another number-one live B-side.

And this brings us back to "Fingertips—Part 2," which was the B-side companion of "Part 1." It's unusual but not out of the ordinary for B-sides to hit number one, with at least ten songs turning the trick. And that's not including double A-side pairings in which each song independently reached the top of the charts, such as Elvis Presley's "Hound Dog" paired with "Don't Be Cruel" and the Beatles' "Something" backed with "Come Together." Included in these overachieving B-sides are the (disputed) first rock-and-roll hit, "(We're Gonna) Rock Around the Clock," the flip side of Bill Haley & His Comets' long-forgotten "Thirteen Women (And Only

One Man in Town)," Gloria Gaynor's disco anthem "I Will Survive," and white-rap punchline Vanilla Ice's "Ice Ice Baby."

Stevie would enjoy only one other top 100 pop B-side, 1971's "Never Dreamed You'd Leave in Summer." It hit number 78 backing a number 13 cover of the Beatles' number-one hit "We Can Work It Out." Wonder performed the B-side at the July 2009 Michael Jackson memorial service.

And for the moment we're all numbered out, Parts 1 and 2.

Chapter One Playlist

"Tiptoe through the Tulips," Nick Lucas

"The Battle of Manassas," John Davis

"Big Girls Don't Cry," The Four Seasons

"My Boyfriend's Back," The Angels

"My Eyes Adored You," Frankie Valli

"Stranger on the Shore," Acker Bilk

"Fly, Robin, Fly," Silver Convention

"When the Rain Begins to Fall," Jermaine Jackson and Pia
   Zadora

"My Ding-a-Ling," Chuck Berry

"Mony Mony (Live)" Billy Idol

"Thirteen Women (And Only One Man in Town)," Bill Haley
   & His Comets

2

"ALFIE"

The Search for Style

In the mid-1970s, Brand Stevie Wonder was easy to identify: Stevie Wonder is a Funk Genius! But for most of the 1960s, Motown banked on Stevie's continued novelty while churning through multiple genres to find songs and an image that clicked with the proper (i.e., white) audiences:

- He's Little Stevie, inheritor to the Ray Charles legacy performing "Don't You Know"!
- He's a suave pop crooner, melting your heart with "When You Wish Upon a Star"!
- He's Annette and Frankie's après-surf pal boppin' down "Happy Street"!
- He's an R&B dynamo—he's "Uptight" (but everything's alright)!

- He's a pensive folk singer, his thoughts "Blowin' in the Wind"!
- He's an easy-listening instrumentalist, lulling you into the dentist's chair with "Alfie"!

This chapter looks at the diversity of styles Stevie explored on his path toward contractual and creative freedom in 1971, with an emphasis on cognitive outliers for twenty-first-century Brand Stevie Wonder. It also looks at how those creative choices intersected with the career paths of multiple contemporaneous performers: In whose image did Motown think they were forging Stevie Wonder?

THE BACKSTORY

"Alfie" (1968) stands as the most incongruous of Wonder's singles: it's an easy-listening instrumental. What? Aside from the up-front harmonica, not much marks this as a "Stevie Wonder" song. And, in fact, it wasn't marked "Stevie Wonder" at all but by his ananym "Eivets Rednow," which also served as the title of the eponymous 1968 LP. The album wasn't even released on the usual Tamla Records but on Gordy, the off-brand outlet for the Temptations and "Super Freak" Rick James.

The song was written by lyricist Hal David and composer Burt Bacharach for Michael Caine's 1966 breakout film *Alfie*. The increasingly cringey swinging-London celebration of male prerogative, directed by frequent James Bond helmsman Lewis Gilbert, had a knockout jazz soundtrack by Sonny Rollins but needed a pop single to hook the kids. The UK film cut got a Liverpool-native Cilla Black version of "Alfie," and the United States got a release from Imperial Valley's favorite daughter, Cher. Cher's version was a follow-up to her number-two single "Bang Bang," which Stevie covered on 1966's *Down to Earth.*

Black's and Cher's versions both reached the top 40 in their respective countries, but Dionne Warwick had the best-known US hit with the song in 1967. By the time Wonder released his take in late 1968, the song had been recorded at least sixty times on the way to almost three hundred recorded versions. The film itself was remade in 2004 with Jude Law in the lead role.

Wonder performed "Alfie" on and off during his career, most notably for the 1973 TV movie *Burt Bacharach: Opus No. 3* and on May 9, 2012, at a Gershwin Award tribute to David and Bacharach. The latter White House event also featured Stevie on the piano for the Walker Brothers' number-one UK hit "Make It Easy on Yourself," with Cuban trumpeter Arturo Sandoval, and accompanied by Bacharach on "What the World Needs Now Is Love."

In addition to "Alfie," Wonder recorded David and Bacharach's "A House Is Not a Home" for the all-instrumental *Eivets Rednow.* Warwick had previously released her version of that track on a 1964 single and her *Make Way for Dionne Warwick* album; Luther Vandross's 1981 epic seven-minute version has climbed Slow Jam Valhalla. The 1964 Warwick LP included a version of the show tune "People," a song Stevie performed at a 2011 MusiCares Barbra

Streisand tribute and recorded with Streisand as a duet in 2014. From all this, you'd think there are only a handful of recordable songs in the world.

Aside from the easy-listening single and the name subterfuge, *Eivets Rednow* is best remembered as the first LP to include Wonder solo compositions. "How Can You Believe" has had the longest legs. Sax player Ari Ambrose released an engaging ten-plus-minute version in 2002 before becoming a New York City–based immigration attorney. The unassuming harmonica track was given further life through a 2004 sample on Madvillain's brilliant "Great Day."

The clavinet-heavy "Which Way the Wind" thinks about being funky but doesn't quite get there.

The Wonder original "Bye Bye World" was originally intended for a collaborative LP with Wes Montgomery. Stevie's keys lay an obvious guide for Montgomery's unique thumb-stroking technique, but the guitarist died before recording it.

ARETHA, DINAH, MARVIN, AND STEVIE

Of course, Stevie wasn't the only otherworldly talented Black performer who experienced these types of growing pains. Columbia spent six years (1960–1966), ten albums, and twenty-odd singles trying to figure what to do with Aretha Franklin and how to do it. They never quite did.

The early Franklin albums, such as her 1961 Columbia debut *Aretha: With the Ray Bryant Combo*, often mirror Stevie's eclectic mid-sixties LPs: a mix of near jazz/R&B ("Sweet Lover"), Broadway tunes ("Are You Sure"), and standards ("Over the Rainbow"). In other words, something like Stevie's *With a Song in My Heart*: an LP that might appeal to Black audiences, but at the very least won't offend white audiences, where the real money is. With that thought in mind, Columbia and Franklin targeted audiences via the recently deceased Dinah Washington on *Unforgettable: A Tribute to Dinah Washington* (1964), typically considered Aretha's best Columbia album.

Washington's truncated career could/did serve as a blueprint for Franklin and Wonder. The first part of her career, from 1944 to 1958, saw tremendous R&B single success, with thirty-nine top 15 hits on Mercury's jazz label EmArcy. Then, in 1958, Washington flowed to Mercury's main label with the album *The Queen* and the single "Make Me a Present of You," and the marketing tides turned. The single only hit number 27 on the R&B chart. And while she would enjoy three more R&B number ones, including two duets with Brook Benton, her future lay in a series of twenty top 100 pop singles. While only three of these tunes broke the top 10 (her signature tune "What a Difference a Day Makes" and the Benton duets "Baby [You've Got What It Takes]" and "A Rockin' Good Way [To Mess Around and Fall in Love]"), this exposure led to Washington in 1959 being the first Black woman to play the Las Vegas Strip, with all the white supper-club money and exposure that entailed. It took Berry Gordy until 1966 to get the Supremes to the Flamingo.

Dinah Washington died on December 14, 1963, at the age of thirty-nine. Columbia and Franklin quickly tried to fill the void, releasing the tribute album just sixty-six days later on February 18, 1964. As David Ritz points out in his definitive Franklin biography, "The marketing men targeted her to a much older audience." But marketing to a much older audience had taken a targeted hit just nine days before when the Beatles appeared on *The Ed Sullivan Show* and demographics trended much younger. So the gears shifted again. Franklin's next album, *Runnin' Out of Fools*, was aimed at a hipper "Sound of Young America" audience, featuring two Motown songs, "Every Little Bit Hurts" and "My Guy." This was the first of three consecutive top-ten R&B albums, although she didn't become the Queen of Soul until a 1967 switch to Atlantic Records and her number-one pop and R&B smash "Respect."

Washington, Franklin, and Wonder share one song: "Teach Me Tonight." Washington's 1954 number 23 is stark, highlighting her hypnotizing vocals. The Grammy Hall of Fame recording is the definitive take among over 250 versions circulating (not that I've listened to all of them). Aretha's version is a pleasant, rolling, twilight tune from 2014's *Aretha Franklin Sings the Great Diva Classics*. Stevie's version is an upbeat, flip-the-switch "Motown song" duet (quintet?) with the Four Tops. Lady Gaga has expressed an interest in recording "Teach Me Tonight" as a duet with Stevie, but it has not happened.

Stevie and Aretha's friendship stretched from the 1960s to 2018, when he and Jesse Jackson were among Aretha's hospice visitors before her death on August 16. Their recording careers intersected several times, also.

According to Franklin biographer Ritz, the two bonded backstage at a Fisk University Student Benefit Concert on May 4, 1971. Franklin told Stevie she admired "It's a Shame," the top 20 hit he wrote for the Spinners, and asked when she'd get her hit from him. He told her he'd already written it: "Until You Come Back to Me (That's What I'm Gonna Do)." She released the flute-driven track as the lead single from *Let Me in Your Life* in late 1973, hitting number one on the R&B charts. Stevie recorded his less plush version in 1967, but it wasn't released until 1977's *Looking Back* compilation.

Prior to that, Wonder finished his version of Otis Redding's "Respect" about four weeks after Franklin's dropped from the top of the pop charts in June 1967. Stevie's version is passable—nice harmonica solo—but he is chasing genius here and doesn't catch up.

In 1974 Aretha covered "I Love Every Little Thing about You" on *With Everything I Feel in Me*. The slinky track doesn't measure up to Stevie's original on 1972's *Music of My Mind*, which mostly sounds like a demo for a late 1970s Michael Jackson album track. But the winner here is Syreeta's funky, proto-disco take from 1972's *Syreeta*, produced by Wonder and associates Malcolm Cecil and Robert Margouleff.

MOTWANG: COUNTRIFIED DETROIT

When we talk about Motown wanting to wish Stevie Wonder upon Ray Charles's star in late 1962, at that point we're talking about Ray

Charles 1.0. In early 1962, Uncle Ray 2.0 made the bold career move to put aside the R&B that had placed him on the charts since 1952 and instead pursue his love of country music. Darius Rucker without the unpleasantness of Hootie and the Blowfish.

The move paid off marvelously. *Modern Sounds in Country and Western Music* hit number one across the charts. *Volume Two* followed to acclaim six months later in October 1962. Charles's lolling, string-heavy covers of Don Gibson's "I Can't Stop Loving You" and "You Are My Sunshine" are the definitive versions of these all-time classics, and the former proved a sonic blueprint for many adult-contemporary-friendly careers, including second-life Elvis Presley and Van Morrison.

Motown incorporated Charles's focus on big orchestration and improving the standards into mid-sixties Stevie records but surprisingly never took an extended, full-tilt plunge into country music. But that doesn't mean Stevie hasn't dabbled in the genre during his career.

Wonder's first try at country was a 1963 cover of Hank Williams's "Your Cheatin' Heart." Charles had a top 30 hit in 1962 with the single from *Volume Two*. It might be the sweetest piece of ear candy ever. Stevie dialed back the singers and orchestration and highlighted the harmonica on his big-band instrumental version.

The Williams track was meant for the unreleased *Workout Stevie, Workout* LP. The Clarence Paul project would have been a mishmash of a few non-hit singles, including the title track, a few Motown originals, along with slick instrumental versions of standards such as "Satin Doll" and "Mack the Knife." The album went unreleased at the time but saw the light of day on 2005's *The Complete Stevie Wonder* digital collection. Instead, Tamla released *With a Song in My Heart*, a vapid collection of ten orchestrated adult contemporary tunes, and *Stevie at the Beach*, a mishmash of a few non-hit singles and lesser instrumental standards. And with this, Stevie's career was at a standstill. Maybe he should have recorded a country album to kick-start his career.

Instead, the country-Motown gimmick album would go to the Supremes, with *Sing Country Western & Pop* in February 1965, an LP sandwiched between the British Invasion tribute *A Bit of Liverpool* and *We Remember Sam Cooke*. Poorly received, it's the least inspiring song collection from the original trio. However, for this story, it does include a cover of Wonder's cowritten "Sunset" from *Tribute to Uncle Ray* (not really a country tune) and the cowritten "Baby Doll," one of the first of about a hundred songs Stevie wrote or cowrote exclusively for another artist.

The Supremes album also includes a cover of Willie Nelson's "Funny How Time Slips Away." Stevie covered the Elvis Presley–associated classic on 1965's *Motortown Revue in Paris*. The original various artists LP also included "High Heel Sneakers" and another version of "Fingertips." The 2016 Deluxe Expanded Edition revealed the exclusive "Jazz-Blues Instrumental" and "Make Someone Happy" from *With a Song in My Heart* (which Aretha covered in 1963).

The plaintive lament "Funny (How Time Slips Away)" seems an oddly mature choice for a fifteen-year-old with seemingly little to plaintively lament. But performed as a duet with Wonder's musical dad Clarence Paul, the song works to frame both the in-the-moment and long-term romantic bruises we all suffer. For all that, the Paris song selections show Stevie musically adrift in 1965: A fifteen-year-old looking back rather than living in the present or looking ahead. But there was hope: "Funny" was quickly pulled as the "High Heel Sneakers" B-side in favor of the more upbeat "Music Talk" from *Up Tight*, Wonder's breakthrough album. "Music Talk" would again turn up as a B-side in 1967 as "Passo Le Mie Notti Qui da Solo" (roughly translated as "I spend my nights alone"), backing the Italian "A Place in the Sun," "Il Sole È Di Tutti."

On February 19, 1969, Stevie appeared on *The Glen Campbell Goodtime Hour*. Campbell was a country-pop crossover singer-songwriter with seven country number-one LPs in the 1960s. Wonder and Campbell sang "Blowin' in the Wind" together, but Stevie started the proceedings with a country goof on "I've Got a Tiger by the Tail," a Buck Owens song that Ray Charles had a hit with in 1965. Owens had provided the impetus for the Beatles' foray into country, with Ringo's cover of the dead-on accurate "Act Naturally."

Of course, Motown had created a label that briefly served as its first de facto country outlet, Mel-o-dy Records. What an odd beast. The label launched in 1962 with the R&B "This Is Our Night" by the Creations, and featured Lamont Dozier's Motown family solo debut, "Dearest One." The country that pops up on this label isn't the sweet, AM-friendly fare of Ray Charles but less-produced "old-time" or "hillbilly" music. The biggest name here is Howard "Don't Call Me Davy" Crockett, who released half a dozen unmemorable singles (to be kind). Crockett, aka Howard Hausey, is best known as writer on several Johnny Horton hits.

Other Mel-o-dy oddities include the pro-war "Sugar Cane Curtain," backed with "Dingbat Diller," by the Chuck-A-Lucks. The Chuck-A-Lucks (the name is a reference to old-time dice shakers) had released a rock-and-roll parody (I hope) called "Disc Jockey Fever" in 1958 that contains some of the worst singing ever committed to vinyl, and, according to unverified sources, the group went on to a lucrative career as hippie-bashing singing comedians in the late 1960s.

And speaking of singing comedians, the label also released the Dickie Goodman–inspired "break-in" record "The Interview (Summit Chanted Meeting)" by "Jack" Haney and "Nikiter" Armstrong. The B-side, "Peaceful" is an instrumental mash-up of "Fever" and "Sixteen Tons," "written" by Motown sales representatives Al Klein and Barney Ales. Klein was also the head of Mel-o-dy Records, which sunk out of sight in 1965 with Crockett's last single, "The Great Titanic."

Motown tried country again in 1974 with the Melodyland label, featuring T. G. Sheppard and Pat Boone—yes, that Pat Boone, the one often considered the whitest man ever to put mouth to microphone. Due to copyright issues, the label morphed into Hitsville Records for 1976 and 1977 before finally bringing the charade to a peaceful ending.

During the time Wonder oversaw his own destiny, the only song that touches country is "I Ain't Gonna Stand for It" from 1980's *Hotter Than July*. The lyrics mimic a stereotypical country "cheatin'" song, and Stevie approximates a drawl for some of the verses—more goofin' on than getting into country. But smart business as country was on the ascent at the time.

Wonder started hanging out with country artists more during the 2010s, as artists like Taylor Swift once again renegotiated the country/pop boundaries. In 2015, Wonder lent harmonica to autotune king Jason Derulo's "Broke," which also featured Kiwi country megastar Keith Urban.

In April 2013, Wonder met up with Hunter Hayes. Calling him "a blessing to country music," Wonder likely felt an affinity for the fellow child prodigy, multi-instrumentalist Hayes, who released his first self-produced music at age nine. As with Stevie and "Fingertips—Part 2" at the top of the pop charts, Hayes's "Wanted" found him the youngest to reach the top of the country singles chart, albeit at age twenty-one. The duo performed "Sir Duke" that year at the American County Music Awards, and Stevie closed the show with a performance of "Signed, Sealed, Delivered I'm Yours," accompanied by country stars such as Blake Shelton and Luke Bryan. Stevie and Hunter teamed up again that month for a medley of "All I Do" and "I Ain't Gonna Stand for It" for "Stevie Wonder Night" on *Dancing with the Stars*.

Chapter Two Playlist

"How Can You Believe," Ari Ambrose

"Great Day," Madvillain

"What a Difference a Day Makes," Dinah Washington

"Until You Come Back to Me (That's What I'm Gonna Do),"
Aretha Franklin

"You Are My Sunshine," Ray Charles

"Baby Doll," The Supremes

"Jazz-Blues Instrumental," Stevie Wonder

"Passo Le Mie Notti Qui da Solo," Stevie Wonder

"This Is Our Night," The Creations

"Disc Jockey Fever," The Chuck-A-Lucks

"Wanted," Hunter Hayes

3

"UPTIGHT (EVERYTHING'S ALRIGHT)"

The Motown Sound

Chronologically corrupt, this chapter makes a U-turn from 1968's "Alfie" and resets the clock at 1963 and a quarter past "Fingertips" o'clock. The spotlight is on "Uptight (Everything's Alright)," Wonder's first hit as a maturing artist (at age fifteen), and his work with unsung lyricist Sylvia Moy and writing partners Ron Miller and Bryan Wells. Sorting through the sixties singles and stopping at "Uptight," we eventually arrive at "Signed, Sealed, Delivered I'm Yours" in 1970, finding Stevie on the cusp of scratching his simmering seven-year itch to do his own work on his own terms.

THE BACKSTORY

After the success of "Fingertips—Part 2," Stevie and Motown/Tamla struggled through seven mostly indistinguishable singles over the next two years hoping to relight the Stevie chart fire. While none of the songs are unpleasant, they all more or less stall while singularly chasing the swinging-live-party groove of the number-one single without adding anything to the equation. Stevie even reminds patrons to tip their servers at one point. (Note: he doesn't—but he might as well—on 1970's *Live at the Talk of the Town,*)

The highest charting and marginally best of the lot is the fourth attempt, 1964's "Hey Harmonica Man," which hit 29 on the pop charts and 5 on R&B. It's a call-and-response between Stevie as the title tooter and background singers, who also get to sing an oddly central four-line bridge. The song would end up on the thankfully brief (24:27) *Stevie at the Beach* LP, as the second of the LP's three singles. The non-LP B-side, "This Little Girl," was much of the same without the hourly employed background singers contributing to the cause.

Of the song, Stevie said in 1970, "Looking back, I didn't really like the way I did 'Harmonica Man' and 'Fingertips' but I know that I was much younger then and didn't really quite grasp what I was doing. I suppose that at the time I must have thought it was good but now I know different."

"Hey Harmonica Man" had been recorded as a promo single the previous year for Mercury's Smash Records by Jo Jo Wail and the Somethings. There is less of a paper trail on the identity of this band than there is on the current whereabouts of my first college roommate. The Jo Jo Wail composer credit for the song is Lou Josie (aka producer Jimmy King), with Marty Cooper getting credit for the B-side, "Wailin' Time." Both receive songwriting credit on the Stevie recording. The duo also cowrote a handful of twang/surf songs around that time, including "Guitar Star" for guitarist Duane

Eddy. Eddy's track is a non-LP follow-up to the single "Water Ski-ing" from the eponymous LP; The LP cover makes a fine aquatic companion to *Stevie at the Beach*.

Lou Josie later made it to royalty Valhalla with the Grassroots' "Midnight Confessions" while Marty Cooper had a long, fascinating career that included a string of novelty records ("Mr. Kazoo Man" and its zany B-side "Dearborn, Michigan") and a stint in the Shacklefords with LA recording legend Lee Hazlewood ("These Boots Are Made for Walking"). How Stevie ended up with a song from these guys is unclear, and the fact that he did points toward dire circumstances: there were rumors that he'd be dropped from Motown if he didn't have a hit.

THE SONG

Sylvia Moy was signed as a recording artist in the early 1960s after being discovered by Marvin Gaye and Motown A&R head Mickey Stevenson. With material such as "Hey Harmonica Man," evidence of a dearth of quality material in the couch cushions at 2648 West Grand Boulevard, she was enlisted as Motown's first female song-writer and apprentice/gopher for producer Henry Cosby. While male writers such as Cosby were assigned musicians, Moy, as a woman, was instead assigned another songwriter. And from this she became Motown's first woman producer and, along with frequent writing partner Cosby, was inducted into the Songwriters Hall of Fame in 2006.

Clarence Paul, Stevie's writer/producer/handler since he signed to Motown, later admitted that by 1965, "I didn't have no hits. I couldn't think of nothing, and he couldn't think of nothing." Soon Cosby and Moy teamed up with Wonder and, in a move that Motown head Berry Gordy ultimately credited with "saving" Stevie's career, wrote "Uptight (Everything's Alright)."

Sources credit Moy with pushing Stevie to remember a riff he had been playing so she could marry her lyrics with his melody for a new song. In the end, she pushed him hard enough that he pretty much remembered the Rolling Stones' summer 1965 chart-topper "(I Can't Get No) Satisfaction," itself Keith Richards's hornless take on a generic Otis Redding song. Released in November 1965, the propulsive, celebratory "Uptight" hit number three on the pop charts and was Stevie's second R&B number one. Stevie's career was saved.

Working with Wonder, usually Cosby, and, occasionally, Stevie's mom, Moy would compose over a dozen songs that ended up on Stevie LPs and singles through 1970, including two R&B number ones, "I Was Made to Love Her" and "Shoo-Re-Doo-Be-Doo-Da-Day," and the strolling 1970 single "Never Had a Dream Come True." Among her other notable work for Motown, she cowrote Marvin Gaye and Kim Weston's "It Takes Two" with Stevenson, then Weston's husband, and penned the Motown workhorse "This Old Heart of Mine (Is Weak for You)" with the label's songwriting geniuses, Holland-Dozier-Holland. The latter song was covered by Rod Stewart for a 1975 single and became a mainstay in his live act.

The original enjoyed a revival after it featured in an episode and on the soundtrack of TV's *Moonlighting* in the mid-1980s, and finally went US pop top ten in 1990 with a Stewart and Ronald Isley duet.

Stewart switched from rock/pop in 2002, reimagining himself as a standards interpreter and emitting five LPs in his *The Great American Songbook* series. *Volume III* (2004) found him crooning Louis Armstrong's "What a Wonderful World" with Stevie on harmonica. *Soulbook* (2009) was heavy on Motown and found Stevie accompanying Sir Rod on the Wonder/Cosby/Moy collaboration "My Cherie Amour."

Moy never released any of her own recordings on Motown. She left the label and moved to Los Angeles in 1973. "And This Is Love" was released the same year on 20th Century Records, two years after its first appearance as a single by Sisters Love, an A&M group composed of former Raelettes, Ray Charles's background singers. By the time of Moy's 1973 release, Sisters Love were in the Motown stable, releasing half a dozen singles but never an LP until the 2010 retrospective collection *With Love*.

Gladys Knight & the Pips also released a version of "And This Is Love" in 1973 on their Motown/Soul LP *Neither One of Us*. This LP came out in March, after the group had departed for Buddah Records. Three months later, a spiteful Motown pulled together *All I Need Is Time*, intended to mess with the erstwhile bubblegum label's new signing. Buddah needn't have worried, as Gladys Knight & the Pips' next release, "Midnight Train to Georgia," was also their most successful chart hit.

"And This Is Love" was cowritten with another former Motown writer, Frederick Long. Long started as an artist on Motown's Soul label, working with Mickey Stevenson. He released Soul's first commercial single, "Devil with the Blue Dress," as Shorty Long. It's a tune made famous by Mitch Ryder and the Detroit Wheels and made immortal by Bruce Springsteen and the E Street Band in their "Detroit Medley," which pairs the Long/Stevenson song with Chuck Berry's "Good Golly Miss Molly" and a changeable selection of other Ryder- and Detroit-focused songs.

Long's biggest hit as a Motown recording artist was 1968's funky "Here Comes the Judge," which hit number eight on the pop charts. It was based on a routine by comedian Pigmeat Markham, who released his own "Here Comes the Judge" around the same time on Chess Records. A completely different song, Markham's single is often credited as the first rap record. It's a thing of beauty.

After tiring of the West Coast, Moy moved back to Detroit, where she assembled her own studio, Masterpiece Sound, in her basement. She would continue writing over the next decade, eventually releasing the disco/Northern Soul single "Major Investment" on Ian Levine's UK-based Nightmare Records in 1989. The same year the DJ/impresario Levine founded Motorcity Records, which released recordings by former Motown artists, including Syreeta and Sisters Love. Moy's slick version of "My Cherie Amour" appeared on the label's 1990 collection *20 Detroit Chartbusters* and over the years on countless bargain-bin UK soul compilations. Moy died in 2017.

"Uptight" was a popular cover song until the turn of the new century when interest seems to have fizzled out. First to the gate was Johnny Rivers in 1966 with his patented "live" version from *And I Know You Wanna Dance*, the same LP that featured his hit "Secret Agent Man." Fast on his heels was Johnny Hallyday (known as the French Elvis but also sort of as the French Johnny Rivers) with the French-language "Les Coups," which is less about being reassured by the girl on the other side of the tracks than about "hits" from love—having a crush. Cover songs were bread and butter for both Rivers and Hallyday, so their interest in the song isn't surprising. The Supremes' interest was likely mandatory. They recorded straightforward group versions in spring 1966 that weren't released until the 2000s, and their groovy, more laidback duet with the Temptations featured on 1969's joint *Together*.

Other versions of note are much less faithful to the original. Bill Cosby had a 1967 number-four pop hit, his highest-charting US single, with the parody "Little Ole Man (Uptight, Everything's Alright)." Although the song featured original lyrics, the music was a note-for-note copy, and all songwriting credit went to Henry (not Bill) Cosby/Moy/Wonder. C. J. Lewis had a UK number 10 with his controversial reggae interpretation "Everything Is Alright (Uptight)," which interpellated the phrase that enthralled London for a few weeks in the July 1994, "Ribidibidoo-badey, ribidibidoo-badey / Ribidibidoo-badey, things 'em alright." The Cosby/Moy/Wonder trio received co-credit with Lewis, as they did eventually on Oasis's "Step Out," in which Noel Gallagher borrows liberally from the original song's chorus. The song had been slated for inclusion on the band's 1995 magnum opus *(What's the Story) Morning Glory?* without proper attribution. Legal heads prevailed, and the song was pulled. "Step Out" was included on expanded reissues with credit going to the trio and Gallagher.

The "Uptight" B-side is most notable for having nothing to do with Prince. The non-LP "Purple Rain Drops" is a slow-dance romance that got some play on Black radio upon release. The song finds the rapidly maturing Stevie workout-Stevie-workouting to stay in a consistent vocal register.

"Uptight" caused a scramble for a new Stevie LP, a result unlikely before the single's fall 1965 success. The resulting *Up-Tight* was released in May 1966, almost a full two years after *Stevie on the Beach*, a lifetime by mid-1960s release standards. The LP collected songs stretching back to 1962 ("Contract on Love" backed by the Temptations), pairing them with newly recorded tracks backed by the Funk Brothers. The LP brought Stevie back to the pop charts (number 33) after a two-LP absence and marks his first appearances on the US R&B (number 2) and UK (number 14) album charts. While he wouldn't return to the UK chart with any consistency until 1972's *Talking Book*, he has more or less been on the US charts ever since this release.

The LP also included the title track's follow-up single, "Nothing's Too Good for My Baby" (written by Cosby, Moy, and Stevenson), which hit number four on the R&B charts, and a cover of Bob Dylan's "Blowin' in the Wind," which hit number nine on the pop single charts (a spot Dylan only bettered four times) and number one on the R&B charts. After the Dylan tune primed the pump on Stevie as social activist, he quickly cut the hymnlike, content-adjacent "A Place in the Sun," cowritten by Motown lyricist Ron Miller, the only white writer on the Motown staff, and composer Bryan Wells. Miller had placed songs with Stevie ("Give Your Heart a Chance" on *With a Song in My Heart*), Marvin Gaye ("Hello Broadway"), and the Supremes ("Twinkle Twinkle Little Me") before he found Wells playing in a bar and tapped him as a new partner based on a series of melodies played by the piano man.

Released in October 1966, "A Place in the Sun" hit number nine pop and number three R&B and further chipped away at Gordy's reluctance to tackle social issues, however obliquely. The tune got further mileage with an Italian version, "Il Sole È Di Tutti" (The sun's for everyone), backed by an Italian version of the *Up-Tight* track "Music Talk," retitled "Passo Le Mie Notti Qui da Solo" (I spend my nights alone).

Miller and Wells's next tune for Stevie, the somewhat maudlin "Some Day at Christmas," was released less than a month after "A Place in the Sun." This 7-inch doubling up for the holiday season wasn't unusual (James Brown released four singles the same November, including three Christmas songs, the best of the lot the equally maudlin "Let's Make Christmas Mean Something This Year"), but the song failed to hit the pop or R&B charts. The Jackson 5 and the Temptations released versions in 1970 on their Christmas albums, but it wasn't until 2004 that the tune gained more widespread recognition when a remastered and expanded CD of the 1967 LP *Someday at Christmas* was rereleased as *The Best of Stevie Wonder* in Motown's 20th Century Masters—The Christmas Collection, and Pearl Jam offered a funky, upbeat version as their 2004 holiday single. Over seventy versions ensued, including takes by Justin Bieber, Stevie and singer/actor Andra Day (for a version that was featured in a 2015 Apple commercial), and Lizzo; the latter two entered the R&B charts.

The now seasonal radio classic was followed three months later by "Travelin' Man," which showed up on *Stevie Wonder's Greatest Hits Vol. 2* and in 1968 as an Italian A-side "Dove Vai?" (literally, Where you goin'?). The song echoes the real-but-abstract social struggles of "Blowin' in the Wind" and "A Place in the Sun." The final Miller/Wells collaboration was "Yester-Me, Yester-You, Yesterday." This was recorded in early 1967 but sat on the shelves until late summer 1969, when Motown once again looked to the vaults to assemble the oddball, mostly forgettable *My Cherie Amour* LP (songs from The Doors? *The King & I*?) to capitalize on the title song, which hit number four on the pop and R&B charts. "Yester-Me, Yester-You, Yesterday" redeems the second side of the LP, but the nostalgic love song is a B-level single. It went top ten on both charts.

Wells left Motown in 1970, working briefly for Bette Midler before joining the commercial music industry. Miller enjoyed further success with Stevie with "For Once in My Life" and "Heaven Help Us All." His last song for (UK) Tamla/Motown was the psychedelic hippie-funk "Green Grow the Lilacs" (an original, not the folk song) by the Originals. It failed to chart, but the group hit R&B number one on their next single, the tender "Baby I'm for Real," written by Marvin Gaye and his wife/the boss's daughter, Anna Gordy Gaye.

"Yester-Me, Yester-You, Yesterday" was Stevie's last call for the sixties, but the Long Sixties for Stevie stretched through 1970 and the August *Signed, Sealed & Delivered* LP. The record is solid, featuring the anthemic number-one R&B title song and Stevie's first solo production credit, but it's not an album in the way that artists like the Beatles and Bob Dylan, or even the Who and the Kinks, were releasing albums—it was a collection of twelve songs written by ten different songwriting teams. Stevie wanted more. And that more was already in the can, his first masterpiece, *Where I'm Coming From*, cowritten with Syreeta Wright, his September bride. The seven-year itch was to be scratched.

Chapter Three Playlist

"Guitar Star," Duane Eddy

"Dearborn, Michigan," Marty Cooper

"This Old Heart of Mine (Is Weak for You)," Rod Stewart

"And This Is Love," Gladys Knight & the Pips

"Devil with the Blue Dress," Shorty Long

"Here Comes the Judge," Pigmeat Markham

"Major Investment," Sylvia Moy

"Les Coups," Johnny Hallyday

"Little Ole Man (Uptight, Everything's Alright)," Bill Cosby

"Everything Is Alright (Uptight)," C. J. Lewis

"Green Grow the Lilacs," The Originals

4

"DO YOURSELF A FAVOR"

Finding the Funk

Stevie Wonder is funky. Very funky. But he gets short shrift in Rickey Vincent's essential-but-hurried bible of funk, *Funk: The Music, the People, and the Rhythm of the One.* The book begins with Stevie justly placed at the right hand of the Godfather: "Artists like Stevie Wonder and George Clinton assumed the role of the avatar of a Black nation's dreams, but the central locus of all funk, the representation of the total and complete Black man, was James Brown." After that, however, Stevie's barely mentioned. We can find him on half a dozen pages highlighting the highs ("You Haven't Done Nothin'") and lows ("That Girl") of socially relevant soul-funk. And he's only just tucked into the "Funky Soul" chapter, with his two-and-a-half page Mr. DeMille spotlight sore-thumbed between a page on the "sex music theme" (Barry White, Sylvia Robinson) and a page-plus on the O'Jays. Backstabbers, indeed.

This isn't meant as an attack on Vincent's book. Appearing in 1996, it was in the right place at the right time (and he does call Dr. John's "Right Place, Wrong Time" "a seething funk monster," speaking truth). And it has a much broader agenda than we have here, which is reckoning Stevie's funk and its place on funk's Mount Rushmore/Tunkasila Sakpe Paha/Six Grandfathers Mountain alongside James Brown and George Clinton.

THE BACKSTORY

Defining "funk" often takes the form of a parlor trick, with definers often using lots of staid terminology to humorously highlight the inability of words to capture the lived and embodied nature of funk. Vincent says, "Funk is impossible to completely describe in words, yet we know funk when we see it," echoing Justice Potter Stewart's 1964 definition of obscenity: "I know it when I see it."

In 1970's "What Is Soul," George Clinton's Funkadelic offer multiple impressionistic definitions for soul that can be read as definitions of funk:

- "Soul is the ring around your bathtub"
- "Soul is a joint rolled in toilet paper"
- "Soul is rusty ankles and ashy kneecaps"
- "Soul is chitlins foo yung"
- "Soul is a ham hock in your cornflakes"

And that ham hock's probably sitting in a bowl of Kellogg's Corn Flakes, fortified with vitamins and minerals. Vitamins that were discovered/invented unbelievably by the Polish chemist Casimir Funk.

I don't think Stevie's soul, or even his funk, approached the glorious stank of Funkadelic (Stevie wasn't snacking on chitlins foo yung) or even Clinton's more user-friendly incarnation as Parliament, but there's no doubt that he tested positive for the funk mo' better and mo' often than most.

WHERE DID THE FUNK START FOR STEVIE?

Stevie was always, by definition, funky, even when Berry Gordy was trying to sell him as a novelty act to white audiences. But this doesn't mean he was always producing funk music. That wouldn't start to happen until the April 1968 release of "Shoo-Re-Doo-Be-Doo-Da-Day." It's not the dead-on double funk of "Licking Stick, Licking Stick" that James Brown was releasing simultaneously, but it's getting there, sacrificing a whole lot of melody and high-end integrity for a whole lotta groove. And it's got that clavinet that would become Stevie's signature funk sound, the 1970s aural equivalent of an Afro pick.

Stevie's other major pre-funk funk was the March 1971's cover of the Beatles' "We Can Work It Out." It's a fuzzed-out romp that Wonder biographer Mark Ribowsky says "ladled on the funk with an anvil."

Two other Motown acts would tackle John and Paul's proto-peace anthem, both producing versions that hit with whatever is the opposite of an anvil. A feather? Valerie Simpson's 1971 version starts as downbeat cocktail jazz before transitioning into a frilly *Hair / Godspell* dance song. The song was produced by Nickolas Ashford, her longtime writing/producing partner and eventual husband. Their biggest hit together was the 1984 R&B number one "Solid." The little-known Fantastic Four recorded a somnambulistic version in 1969 that remained unheard until 2015's *The Lost Motown Album—With Bonus Tracks from the Vaults*, a reimagining of their unreleased *How Sweet He Is* LP.

Tellingly, Stevie's version of the Beatles' eleventh pop number one is almost a whole minute longer than the original. And that extra time is used to stretch out, with less concern for tight Motown structure and more interest in generating that ring around your bathtub.

And stretching out is what would make the funk for Stevie. Only three studio LP tracks extended beyond five minutes before 1971's *Where I'm Coming From*, on which three of the nine tracks went beyond five minutes. And those earlier, longer songs weren't the pick of the litter.

The Cosby-Paul instrumental "Some Other Time," from the debut *The Jazz Soul of Little Stevie*, stretches out for all of 5:11. It's somber Left Bank jazz that's poorly recorded and shrill—a rough listen.

"Make Someone Happy" from the Broadway musical *Do Re Mi* appeared on 1966's *With a Song in My Heart*, Motown's last full-throttle attempt to get Stevie booked regularly on the Las Vegas

Strip. At 5:04, it's an overlong showcase for the dying embers of Stevie's adolescent vocals and better handled more succinctly in the era by Aretha Franklin and swinging Bobby Darin. It is a song much loved by grandmothers.

"Ruby" was written by famed lyricist Mitchell Parish ("Star Dust" "Sleigh Ride") with composer Heinz Roemheld for the 1952 King Vidor film *Ruby Gentry*. Stevie recorded it as a very, very long 6:48 instrumental on *Eivets Rednow*, an LP that Ribowsky describes as a "nine-song sedative." It's frustrating that Wonder never recorded the song with vocals or verve, and his arrangement almost seems like an ironic retort to Ray Charles's concise 1960 single, which hit number 10 on the R&B chart.

So, when did Stevie have the nerve to stretch it out and really get funky?

THE SONG

Stevie rips the Band-Aid off the three-minute Motown pop song on *Where I'm Coming From*'s 6:10 calling card "Do Yourself a Favor." It's the second track on the LP, after the slight "Look Around." The song features Stevie's wah-wah clavinet jamming in and out of call-and-response choruses, backed by a monster synth bass and acres of freewheelin' jammin'. It's not quite LP versions of "Super Bad" or "Hot Pants" at nine-plus minutes, but it's getting there.

But the funk also resides in the lyrics, co-credited to Syreeta Wright. They list a litany of all the bad things going down—garbage, death, Lucifer, poison, a thorny mule (a thorny mule?). It is majorly funky out there, and Stevie's angry about it. But brother, there's a solution: Stevie more sensibly admonishes the listener to "do yourself a favor / educate your mind." This angry-but-conciliatory Stevie is a mainstay of his funk oeuvre.

In addition to being Stevie's hard right into funk, according to Will Fulton in his doctoral dissertation "Reimagining the Collective: Black Popular Music and Recording Studio Innovation, 1970–1990," following Craig Werner, this song "could truly be seen as a 'rough draft' for his new musical direction in terms of Wonder's multitracked one-man band performance, his representation of jamming interaction, and sonic experimentation." In other words, this song, featuring Stevie "playing with himself," is the prototype for the recording practices of the Classic Albums period.

Fulton continues, "The spontaneous interaction between instruments and voices which occurs in a group of musicians performing together is therefore displaced. It is transformed into an organized, technologically facilitated series of reactions, which occur over a period of time as Wonder responds to his performances prerecorded on tape." He's a one-man band.

A few other artists had done this before, most notably Paul McCartney on his 1970 debut as a solo performer, *McCartney*. But McCartney quickly retreated to the comfort of a working band (on 1971's *Ram*) from which he had emerged, returning to solitary status again only on 1980's *McCartney II* and the 2020 COVID-lockdown-necessitated *McCartney III*. By contrast, Stevie would push himself to explore the possibilities of one-person recording for the next half decade.

"Do Yourself a Favor" was covered twice on LP. In 1972 Edgar Winter's White Trash released a live version on their two-disc *Roadwork*, recorded in part at the Apollo Theater. The music is loud and funky, but Winter's arena-rock yelling is difficult to take. Winter's pop number-one instrumental "Frankenstein" is hard/prog-rock heading toward funk, authentic enough for Prince to often work it into his live sets from 2009 onward.

Ocean Colour Scene, part of the early 1990s Britpop wave that included Blur and Oasis, released a version as the fourth single from their self-titled debut album in 1992. It's a guitar-heavy interpretation featuring Steve Cradock, who has concurrently been UK legend Paul Weller's guitarist since 1992. *Innervisions* is one of Weller's top five favorite albums of all time.

The other occasionally funky tune on Stevie's Big Boy Pants LP, *Where I'm Coming From*, is "I Wanna Talk with You," which reads like a Beatles or Prince tongue-in-cheek non-LP B-side. The album did have two solid singles—both ballads. "Never Dreamed You'd Leave in Summer" was first the "We Can Work It Out" B-side before rising to number 78 on the pop charts on its own.

The other single was "If You Really Love Me," top ten pop and R&B, one of the last old-time Motown tunes from Stevie. It was released in July 1971, about two months after Stevie's May 31 birthday. All birthdays are special, but this was Stevie's twenty-first and, as such, the day he came of age and could break free of Motown. And after receiving his coming-of-age royalty check for $100,000, only $3.3 million short of what his newly hired lawyer thought he was owed, he did break free, voiding his contract. After a few months of negotiations, including flirting with other labels, Stevie re-signed with Motown, but with complete creative control, production and publishing rights, and major bank. He won the battle.

"If You Really Love" was one of the last songs Wonder would record at Hitsville in Detroit. During the time between his birthday and his summer 1971 re-signing with Motown, Stevie decamped to New York City and took up residence at Electric Lady Studio. There he would record *Music of My Mind* and *Talking Book*, the first two of his five all-time classic albums that would be released from 1972 to 1976.

FUNKY EPILOGUE

Rickey Vincent puts James Brown as the funk godfather, with Stevie and George Clinton as his direct descendants. How did Stevie and Motown mingle with these two giants?

James Brown never recorded for the Motown label (unless he used one of his dozens of pseudonyms and no one knows it), but he did go out on a Motortown Revue. According to Brown in his autobiography, which is often mostly accurate, in 1962 Berry Gordy approached his manager to help Motown "get a better foothold in the business." James headlined the Motortown Revue for a spell, playing with the Miracles, the Supremes, Marvin Gaye, and others, including "Little Stevie Wonder, who was only twelve years old at the time." A few years later, Brown would share the spotlight with the Miracles, the Supremes, and Marvin Gaye (and the Rolling Stones) at the legendary TAMI (Teenage Awards Music International) Show.

Stevie recorded James's "Please Please Please" on his cover-heavy 1967 LP *I Was Made to Love Her*. And a few years later, in 1972, he got grumpy about Brown:

> I mean this isn't exactly a criticism but James Brown said he'd retire four years ago and like he's been going on stage and doing the same thing over and over again ever since Me, I'd get tired of that, because after a while people are bound to say "man I'm sick of that shit."

This quote aged about as well for Stevie as Mick Jagger saying, "I'd rather be dead than sing 'Satisfaction' when I'm 45." As of this writing, Jagger was seventy-nine at his most recent performance of "Satisfaction" and Stevie seventy-four at his last performance of "For Once in My Life."

Stevie and James didn't play together but would later share a stage (*the* stage) at the May 4, 1985, Motown Tribute to the Apollo Theater. James did "Please Please Please." Stevie did four songs, including an unexpected pairing with Boy George on "Part-Time Lover."

James Brown also pinch-hit for Stevie on the 1973 soundtrack to director Larry Cohen's *Black Caesar*. According to Cohen:

> We first tried Stevie Wonder. He came to the screening. He's blind, of course, and couldn't see the picture but he could hear it. He thought it was a little too violent for him. The next one on the list was James Brown.

It's difficult to think of Stevie scoring *Black Caesar* or any blaxploitation film. But then again, it's often difficult to remember that he created the vegsploitation score *Stevie Wonder's Journey through "The Secret Life of Plants."*

It's not known if James Brown ever thought that Stevie Wonder should get off the stage. But we know that Clinton wanted to "take it to the stage" and, from Parliament's 1975 classic "Chocolate City," that he thought that JB should be the vice president of the United States (to Muhammad Ali's POTUS) and that Stevie should be secretary of fine arts.

George Clinton began his musical career in the late 1950s in Plainfield, New Jersey, as the leader of the vocal group the Parliaments, a barbershop quintet formed in the backroom of a literal barbershop. The group released their first single, "Poor Willie / Party Boys," on ABC-Paramount subsidiary label APT Records in 1959. It's harmony vocals over a "Stand by Me" stutter bass. Their subsequent single, 1960's "Lonely Island / (You Make Me Wanna) Cry," was released on Flipp Records. Neither 7-inch charted.

Standing somewhat distant from the verge of getting it on, the Parliaments drifted toward Detroit and Motown. As Clinton recalls,

> It was like being out at your high school, opening day, everybody out on the lawn and you recognizing these people from their stars. That's Stevie Wonder. That's The Temptations. That's right when they had their Motown review going around the world. So they all was there early this morning and we looking out the cars like little kids. So that blew our mind.

The Parliaments recorded at least two songs for Motown in late 1963/early 1964. "You're Not Hurting Him (You're Hurting Me)" survives as an acetate and circulates in a snippet on a YouTube video. Clinton wrote the song with Motown writers Stanley Ossman ("I Can Take a Hint" for the Miracles) and George Kerr, who doesn't seem to have any official Motown writing credits. The group also recorded "Misjudged You," written by Clinton with longtime partner Ernie Harris ("Can You Get to That") and Parliament-Funkadelic legend Clarence "Fuzzy" Haskins. Neither of these recordings have been officially released, although the latter was rerecorded and found a home as the sweet song "I Misjudged You" on Parliament's 1975 classic *Chocolate City*.

Ultimately, the group was rejected by Motown. According to Clinton, the reason for the rejection was that the group was too short in comparison with combos like the Temptations and the Four Tops. And too funky is more like it.

Although his group didn't make the cut at the time, Clinton continued writing for Motown's Jobete Publishing. He is purported to have had a hand in writing at least thirty songs for Jobete, although it's unclear how many of these were actually recorded and how many survive in any form. Records indicate that girl group the Parlettes recorded a few songs, including the Clinton-penned "If It Were True." The Parlettes trio included Tamala Lewis, a Clinton songwriting partner and mother of his now-deceased son, P-Funk mainstay Tracey Lewis aka Trey Lewd.

Released Clinton Motown songs that carry the Jobete name include "Can't Shake It Loose" by Diana Ross and the Supremes (1968's *Love Child*) and "I'll Bet You" by the Jackson 5 (1970's *ABC*). Both were scheduled for release on a 1969 Funkadelic Westbound Records single that was canceled; both ultimately appeared on the essential 1992 compilation *Music for Your Mother—Funkadelic 45s*. Michael Jackson recorded "Little Christmas Tree," which ended up on 1973's *A Motown Christmas*.

Additionally, at least half a dozen Clinton Jobete songs ended up being recorded by non-Motown artists, such as Roy Handy's 1965 single "Baby That's a Groove," cowritten with Holland and Dozier, and the Pets' "I Say Yeah" (1965).

More or less shunned by Motown, the Parliaments released the single "Heart Trouble (Without Your Love) / That Was My Girl" on Detroit's Golden World label in 1967 before moving to Detroit's Revilot Records. The group's first and only hit on the label was their first single for Revilot, the gospel-tinged "(I Wanna) Testify."

Parliament would funk up the song on 1974's *Up for the Down Stroke*. Seventeen of the group's Revilot songs ended up on various compilation CDs in the 1990s.

The last Revilot single, "A New Day Begins / I'll Wait" was released in 1968, the same year Rose Williams with George Clinton and the Funkadelics released the tame "Whatever Makes My Baby Feel Good." But the true and glorious funk revolution would begin in 1969 with Funkadelic's "I'll Bet You / Qualify and Satisfy," Temptations psychedelia pushed an extra step, backed with Zeppelin-heavy blues. The funk gauntlet was thrown down.

Chapter Four Playlist

"Right Place, Wrong Time," Dr. John

"What Is Soul," Funkadelic

"Licking Stick, Licking Stick," James Brown

"Solid," Ashford & Simpson

"Do Yourself a Favor," Edgar Winter's White Trash

"Chocolate City," Parliament

"Poor Willie," The Parliaments

"I Can Take a Hint," The Miracles

"I Misjudged You," Parliament

"Can't Shake It Loose," Diana Ross and the Supremes

"Qualify and Satisfy," Funkadelic

5

"SUPERSTITION"

Rock Star Status

Stevie Wonder is a Rock Star, but it would be a stretch to call him a Rocker or a Rock-and-Roller or whatever increasingly antiquated term is associated with acts such as, to echo the Clash in "1977," Elvis, Beatles, the Rolling Stones. But he is in the Rock & Roll Hall of Fame (so is XXX!—name your crazy inclusion and stupid omission). And he's often dipped his toes in at the periphery of what's happening in the rock scene, even if he rarely dove in headfirst.

This chapter reviews some of those times that Stevie crossed paths with the rock world, with a closer look at the creation of one of his most rocking (and funky) songs, "Superstition." The point of this chapter isn't necessarily to ponder what might have been had he veered off in a slightly harder direction, although that's a subtext, but more to consider further Stevie's (and Motown's) place in the larger music firmament. It's more about the Ecology of Stevie

Wonder than Stevie as an individual organism: Goes to 11's Journey into the Secret Life of Stevie Wonder.

THE BACKSTORY

Stevie started recording at Motown in 1962 and by the time his first hit, "Fingertips—Part 2," topped the US charts in mid-1963, the pop music game was bending toward rock and "beat" music as the Beatles topped the UK charts.

The Beatles had a long relationship with Stevie and Motown. The group dove into Motown on their second official LP, *With the Beatles* (1963) in the UK and *The Beatles' Second Album* (1964) in the United States. They didn't cover any Stevie songs, but they did record the Marvellettes' "Please Mr. Postman" (with John Lennon's "Deliver de-letter, de-sooner, de-better" an aural marvel), the Miracle's "You Really Got a Hold on Me," and Motown's first hit, Barrett Strong's "Money (That's What I Want)." Lennon performed a gloriously sloppy version of the latter with the Plastic Ono Band featuring Eric Clapton on guitar at the Toronto Rock and Roll Revival 1969, later released as *Live Peace in Toronto*.

Likewise, Motown would pay homage to the Beatles, with artists covering more than a dozen tracks, from the Four Tops' "Eleanor Rigby" to the Supremes' "Come Together" to Syreeta's "She's Leaving Home," produced by Stevie.

Stevie's cover of the Beatles' "We Can Work It Out" is often considered the quintessential Fab Four cover. Wonder hasn't committed any further Beatles songs to vinyl, although he, Henry Crosby, and Sylvia Moy cribbed "Michelle" for "My Cherie Amour." But he's covered the Fab Four in concert, periodically, if only in passing, most notably "Day Tripper," "Michelle," and "She Loves You."

Unlike the Rolling Stones, who made it a point in 1964 to pay homage and record at Chicago's Chess Studios, the Beatles never recorded at Motown. Wonder didn't meet any Beatles until the early morning of February 3, 1966, when Paul McCartney showed up at Stevie's gig at the Scotch of St. James club in London. As with Rick and Louis in *Casablanca*, this was the beginning of a beautiful friendship.

It's unclear when Stevie first met John Lennon, but their paths crossed a few times. Stevie was on the bill at two Lennon led benefit concerts. Along with fellow Detroit native Bob Seger, he played at the John Sinclair Freedom Rally on December 10, 1971, at the University of Michigan. The next year Stevie would perform, alongside Sha Na Na and Roberta Flack, at the Lennon/Ono August 30 One to One concert in New York City to benefit the Willowbrook State School for Retarded (*sic*) Children.

The NYC concert was brought together by reporter Geraldo Rivera. Rivera was also one of the ABC reporters that broke the news of John Lennon's murder during the December 8, 1980, *Monday Night Football* telecast. Stevie watched the news backstage at his Oakland Coliseum concert and went onstage to announce the shocking news.

Stevie participated in the only post-Beatles recording of John and Paul while they were in the same room (discounting the post-John studio mash-ups such as "Free as a Bird"). Released on bootleg as *A Toot and a Snore in '74*, Paul and Linda McCartney visited John Lennon at the Burbank Studios on March 28 as he was producing Harry Nilsson's *Pussy Cats* LP. This was during Lennon's "Lost Weekend" separation from Yoko Ono—two years of drugs, booze, and May Pang.

Stevie wandered into this and sat in on electric piano, with Lennon on lead vocals and guitar and McCartney on drums, with assorted others filling out the sound. The group ran through standards such as "Lucille" and "Stand by Me" as Lennon struggled to control his use of controlled substances (hence the bootleg title). I wish I could say it's a glorious mess and worth a listen, but it's just a mess.

And speaking of messy situations, around the same time, also in Los Angeles, Stevie accompanied George Harrison to dinner with Led Zeppelin. As a practical joke, the members of Led Zeppelin arrived at the dinner in drag, having done so for a recent photo shoot. The visual gag went over with Stevie like a lead balloon. The band was deeply embarrassed, believing that Stevie might have thought they were making fun of his blindness.

It's unclear if Stevie and Ringo Starr ever hung out, although they would have met on multiple occasions, such as 1992's "Bobfest," the Madison Square Garden 30th Anniversary Concert Celebration of Bob Dylan, and in 2015 when they shared a stage for Ringo's solo Rock & Roll Hall of Fame induction. They both appeared on Eddie Vedder's 2022 LP *Earthling*, but not on the same song.

NEIL YOUNG AND RICK JAMES

The Mynah Birds, Motown's white Canadian rock band, featured future Buffalo Springfield members guitarist Neil Young and bassist Bruce Palmer and were fronted by the Black singer Ricky James Matthews. The band played Toronto clubs in 1965 and, through connections, were signed to Motown and placed under the tutelage of Smokey Robinson.

Young says that "Detroit heavies" wandered in and out of their 1966 recording sessions. At some time during recording, not-so-heavy Detroit heavy Stevie Wonder wandered by and convinced Matthews (already a pseudonym), to shorten his name to Ricky James. It was eventually further shortened to Rick James, who would release over twenty top 40 R&B hits for Motown's Gordy label, including the number ones "You and I," "Give It to Me Baby," and "Cold Blooded."

But James's Motown success didn't come until 1978, after a few failed singles on other labels and a stint at the Portsmouth (New Hampshire) Naval Prison.

The Mynah Birds were managed by Morley Shelman. Shelman took off with the band's $25,000 advance, which promptly went into his arm. According to journalist Nick Warburton, the band fired Shelman for the infraction. Shelman, seeking revenge, let Motown know that Matthews/James was AWOL from the U.S. Navy. The band had no idea. According to the demographically challenged Palmer, "We thought he was Canadian, even though there are no Negros in Canada." Motown convinced James to turn himself in as they shelved the band's debut single, "It's My Time."

In addition to the unreleased single, the group recorded at least three other songs for Motown, "Go on and Cry," "I Got You (In My Soul)," and "I'll Wait Forever." All were credited to Ricky Matthews, Michael Valvano, and R. Dean Taylor, except the latter, which was also written by Neil Young. Valvano and the Canadian Taylor were white writers that Motown teamed up with the mostly white Mynah Birds.

Valvano had worked with Wonder and Clarence Paul on Stevie's sixth single, 1964's "Pretty Little Angel," which was also released by Edwin Starr on 1969's *25 Miles*. But he's perhaps best known as the foot stomper on the Supremes' "Baby Love." Taylor never wrote with Wonder but was a longtime scribe and co-author of Diana Ross and the Supremes' pop and R&B number one "Love Child." He also enjoyed success as an artist on Motown's Rare Earth, becoming the first white Motown performer to hit number one on the *Cash Box* charts with 1970's "Indiana Wants Me."

Ricky Matthews had one more pre-James credit for Motown, as cowriter of "Out in the Country" on Bobby Taylor's 1969 *Taylor Made*. Although it may have come as a shock to Bruce Palmer, Taylor was a Black Canadian.

All Mynah Bird tracks were officially released in the 2000s on Motown collections and Neil Young's *The Archives Vol. 1 1963–1972* (2009).

Stevie played harmonica on James's "Mr. Policeman" from the 1981 Gordy label smash *Street Songs*. It's reggae-lite that thematically recalls "Living for the City." Stevie sang "I Won't Complain" (aka "I've Had Some Good Days") at James's 2004 funeral service.

THE SONG

The creation of "Superstition" for 1972's *Talking Book* is inextricably intertwined with producers Robert Margouleff and Malcolm Cecil and English guitarist Jeff Beck.

A week after he turned twenty-one on May 13, 1971, Stevie decamped to New York City. Record shopping a few weeks later, he came across a trippy electronic record by TONTO's Expanding Head Band, *Zero Time*. Stevie was blown away.

The *Zero Time* liner notes indicated that "all sounds on this album are of electronic origin performed on an expanded Series III Moog Synthesizer. All selections on this album were programmed, performed and engineered by Margouleff & Cecil." Intrigued, Stevie tracked down the duo, who worked a few blocks away from where he was staying. He wanted to see TONTO.

TONTO, an acronym for The Original New Timbral Orchestra, was the turducken of synthesizers, a Moog synth augmented by ARP and Oberheim synths and knobs and jacks and boards, oh, my! It took up the entire room of a converted church, was occasionally stuffed in a U-Haul and trucked around New York City, and could do just about anything electronic other than send a man to the moon. Past intrigued, Stevie was smitten.

Still without a recording contract, Stevie began working with Margouleff and Cecil. Flitting between the TONTO room and nearby Mediasound and Electric Lady Studios, and, eventually, Crystal Industries Studios in Los Angeles, he completed *Music of My Mind*. It was the first of four consecutive classic Stevie albums that would include Margouleff and Cecil as associate producers, most likely shortchanging their contributions in the process.

Crystal Industries is now Smash Mouth ("All Star"—sorry I reminded you of the song) producer Eric Valentine's Barefoot Recording Studios. Studio B includes a beautiful marquetry (sort of a wooden mosaic) inspired by Stevie's *Secret Life of Plants*, which was in part recorded at/mixed in Crystal Industries.

While Stevie recorded *Music of My Mind* with the help of just two additional musicians, trombonist Art Baron on the funk classic "Love Having You Around" and guitarist Buzz Feiten on "Superwoman," the recording of *Talking Book* was a more worldly affair employing something approaching a full band. One of those additional musicians was former Yardbirds guitarist Jeff Beck, who had recently met Wonder at a gig at Detroit's Cobo Hall and had engaged Margouleff and Cecil as producers at the same time.

Hanging around the sessions, Beck fell for the slinky-funky "Maybe Your Baby" and asked to record it. Stevie wanted to hold on to it and instead offered a developing song called "Very Superstitious." There are differing stories about Beck's involvement in the evolution of this—He played the drums! He created the intro!—but after Beck's death in 2023, Stevie claimed that Beck's first listen was to a finished version of the song.

Wonder gets full songwriting credit, and the only other musician credits are Steve Madaio on trumpet and Trevor Lawrence on tenor saxophone. Lawrence was married to Lynda Lawrence, at the time a member of the ever changing Supremes and the stand-out female voice on Stevie's "Signed, Sealed, Delivered I'm Yours."

Beck recorded the song with his short-lived trio Beck, Bogert & Appice. Tim Bogert and Carmine Appice had previously found success as the rhythm section of Vanilla Fudge, purveyors of the sludgy psychedelic FM radio staple cover of the Supremes hit "You Keep Me Hangin' On."

Stevie recorded the newly titled "Superstition" at Electric Lady, enveloped by all the mind-blowing psychedelic lights that Jimi Hendrix had installed to create a groovy vibe. The recording was, of course, one of the most amazing things ever, and Motown was eager to release it as a single.

"But we promised it to Jeff Beck."

"This is 'Superstition' by Stevie Wonder. We can't do that."

"OK. You tell him."

"No, you tell him."

Eventually someone told Beck, and neither he nor his label, Epic Records, were happy.

For all the back-and-forth, *Beck, Bogert & Appice* with "Superstition" wasn't released until the spring of 1973, long after Wonder's October 1972 single. And it wasn't that great. And Margouleff and Cecil didn't produce the LP (although the former mastered the Quadrophonic mix).

Beck ended up on one *Talking Book* track, "Lookin' for Another Pure Love," but his solo on "Tuesday Heartbreak" was cut. Despite some animosity, Stevie gave Beck two tracks for his near-perfect debut solo album, 1975's *Blow by Blow*. Stevie wrote the instrumental "Thelonious" and allegedly appears on clavinet. He also let Beck use "Cause We've Ended as Lovers," originally on 1974's *Stevie Wonder Presents Syreeta*. Arguably, the beautiful "Cause We've Ended as Lovers" ended up as Beck's signature song.

"Superstition" would go on to become Stevie's first pop and R&B number one in eleven years. It earned two Grammys and regularly places on lists of the greatest songs of all time. It's been performed live by scores of artists. Many of these artists are guitarists, such as Slash, Joe Satriani, and Stevie Ray Vaughan and owe as much to Beck's version as Wonder's.

By some accounts, "Superstition" is Wonder's most played live track. The definitive non-studio version was performed on the April 12, 1973, episode of the PBS kids' show *Sesame Street*. It's almost seven minutes of eyebrow-raising funk—they let kids near this stuff? Music theorists Paul Fleet and Jonathon Winter point out drummer Ollie E. Brown's work here as especially notable, as he "maintains a four-on-the-floor bass drum and, in different sections of the piece (initially to accompany the entry of the horn riff), plays continuous off-beat open hi-hat resulting in the fully evolved 'disco groove.'" Not that Stevie and Brown invented disco, but they put the record in the groove with this song.

The episode also includes the burning opening song, "1 2 3 Sesame Street," with vocoder and a slight take on "Dancing in the Street," and Stevie having a long talk with Muppet monster Grover ("Have a Talk with Grover?"), trying to teach him to scat on "Don't You Worry 'bout a Thing."

It was also in 1974 that Jeff Beck almost joined the Rolling Stones. Guitarist Mick Taylor, who had replaced Brian Jones in 1969, announced in December that he was quitting. Among others, Beck was considered as a replacement. He was surreptitiously auditioned, but the job went to Beck's Jeff Beck Group bassist Ron Wood. It's a matter of debate if Beck rejected the band or the other way around, with Beck claiming he didn't join because he didn't want to have to punch Keith Richards in the face while recording every album and Keith claiming Beck was rejected because he was too much of an individualist. Oh, boys!

Coincidentally, the Stones were mixing their version of Stevie's "I Don't Know Why" on July 3, 1969, when they received the call that Brian Jones was dead. Stevie had released the single in January, and it reached number 16 on the R&B charts. The Stones were test-driving songs for their *Let It Bleed* LP, which ended up with the more bluesy/country flavor and the Robert Johnson tune "Love in Vain." "I Don't Know Why" wasn't released by the Stones until it appeared on the 1975 odd bits collection *Metamorphosis* and as a single, hitting number 42 on the US pop charts.

By 1975, the Stones were onto their greatest hits Tour of the Americas '75. It was their first US tour since their 1972 jaunt in support of *Exile of Main Street*, which featured Stevie as the opening act. Stevie took the gig for increased exposure to white audiences but ended up getting exposed to the whims of the Stones at the bargain price of $1,000 per gig. How'd that happen?

Motown barely supported *Music of My Mind*, mainly because they felt it didn't have any strong singles (they were right). Wonder had no management at the time. Enter lawyer Johanan Vigoda, who had been negotiating for Margouleff and Cecil and ended up working with Wonder for decades. Vigoda and Cecil called in some favors and got Stevie booked as the opener for the Stones tour.

Vigoda was the judge on "Living for the City." After Vigoda's death in 2011, his wife filed a lawsuit claiming that Wonder owed Vigoda a 6 percent fee of his earnings "forever." The two settled out of court in 2017.

On the Stones tour, Wonder blew the doors off the building every night, whipping the crowd into a frenzy when he was only supposed to warm them up. This infuriated the Stones, who were 90 percent sex and drugs and chaos and only 10 percent rock and roll on this tour. Take a look at the unreleased tour film *Cocksucker Blues*, just not with kids in the room. Some of what went down on tour: Stevie argued with Keith, Mick demeaned Stevie and his race, Stevie's drummer quit, threats were made to kick Wonder and his band Wonderlove off the tour. When things weren't going well, it's reported that the Stones limited Wonder to fifteen-minute sets.

Relations between Stevie and the Stones subsided to low-key hostile levels near the end of the fifty-date trek. By the time of the tour-ending three nights at Madison Square Garden, Stevie was regularly joining the Stones onstage for an encore medley of "Uptight (Everything's Alright)" and "(I Can't Get No) Satisfaction." Their paths crossed over the next fifty years, with Stevie finally joining the remnants of the Stones, along with Lady Gaga, on the gospel-tinged "Sweet Sounds of Heaven" from the band's 2023 LP *Hackney Diamonds*.

Chapter Five Playlist

"1977," The Clash

"Money (That's What I Want)," Plastic Ono Band

"Eleanor Rigby," The Four Tops

"I'll Wait Forever," The Mynah Birds

"Indiana Wants Me," R. Dean Taylor

"Out in the Country," Bobby Taylor

"Mr. Policeman," Rick James

"Thelonious," Jeff Beck

"Cause We've Ended as Lovers," Jeff Beck

"I Don't Know Why," The Rolling Stones

"Sweet Sounds of Heaven," The Rolling Stones

6

"BOOGIE ON REGGAE WOMAN"

Harmonica Man

At the point of this writing, Stevie Wonder has enjoyed a sixty-two-year long career. *Fulfillingness' First Finale* came out in 1974, which means the first half of this book covers a dozen years while the second half covers half a century. Seems unbalanced, but when considering the historically short shelf life of creative genius (save for a few outliers, like Picasso or Miles Davis), it's not unexpected.

Fulfillingness' First Finale has always been an alliterative mouthful, but it's also an uncannily accurate title. Stevie wanted to release it as a double LP, but a contract with total creative control didn't mean total production and marketing control. As a result, the album was released as a single disc, with the implication that there would be a second part at some time. The finale was for his first adult recording contract and the first phase of his "solo" career (*Music of My Mind, Talking Book, Innervisions*). Intentionally or not, he used the LP to finale (to coin a verb) working with his studio associates Robert Margouleff and Malcolm Cecil.

The highlight of *Fulfillingness' First Finale* is "Boogie on Reggae Woman." It's a fun, looping, Escher-like maze of a groove that displays Stevie's instrumental diversity and highlights his signature instrument, the harmonica.

THE BACKSTORY

Stevie started working with Robert Margouleff and Malcolm Cecil around May 1971. For the next four albums, through 1974's *Fulfillingness' First Finale*, the duo would "associate" produce, engineer, program, and generally serve as a sounding board and repository for Stevie's most fecund musical period. By the time they parted ways, Cecil estimated that Wonder had collected over 250 songs for future use.

At the center of the trio's relationship was the duo's TONTO (The Original New Timbral Orchestra) synthesizer. TONTO pulled together a mind-boggling and ever-changing array of synthesizers into one mostly movable unit. According to Cecil, *new timbral* "means each note you play has a different tone quality, as if the notes come from separate instruments." Along the same lines, or maybe contradicting, Margouleff has mentioned that "this is not one instrument, it's all instruments at the same time." There are fascinating online clips of the duo talking about and demonstrating TONTO.

According to the duo, TONTO initially appealed to Stevie less as an instrument and more as a repository and transmitter of ideas. Wonder was overflowing with musical ideas (the "music of my mind"), but the process of communicating those ideas to an arranger and sharing with other musicians was difficult. TONTO gave Stevie the power to control his musical destiny, to show his ideas to people rather than to simply tell them about them.

For all the contemporary discussion of TONTO as the central element of Stevie's musical development at this time, the instrumental array didn't totally dominate Wonder's work on the string of four LPs, at least according to the credits.

TONTO is credited on four *Music of My Mind* songs: "Superwoman," "Girl Blue," "Seems So Long," and "Evil." As a group, these songs are more downbeat and atmospheric than the rest of the album, as if Stevie at this point is using the new instrument to tentatively and sensitively externalize the previously uncharted and uncommunicated territory of his mind. Deep, huh? This is most apparent on "Girl Blue," in which the synthesizer effects create an otherwise impossible soundscape for aching, modulated vocals. This isn't Auto-Tune to get the pitch perfect but synthetic alternation to get the mood right.

There are three TONTO songs on *Talking Book*. "You and I (We Can Conquer the World)" picks up on the pensive mood of the previous tunes, with synthetic mood swirls (that's what I'll call them) providing aural ephemera in a space that's actively constructing future regret ("someone / That may not be here forever"). "You've Got It Bad Girl" is slightly more upbeat, while "Blame It on the Sun" is gospelly and, without the multitimbral modulations, would fit well on earlier, straightforward Motown albums.

On *Innervisions*, the album-closing "He's Misstra Know-It-All" goes full-on gospel with the help of TONTO. It's the least intrusive TONTO song, as the machine is used more as an instrument than as a toy—it's less gimmicky. This is also because Wonder was now including other musicians on the tracks. This track features bassist Willie Weeks, a longtime session man who got his start with the Twin Cities prog-rock band Gypsy and has played with almost everyone, including extended stints with George Harrison, Vince Gill, and Wynonna Judd.

"Golden Lady" also includes other musicians to complement the synthesizer bank—almost a full live band! Clarence Bell, who later recorded as a gospel sideman, was on Hammond organ, Wonderlove member Ralph Hammer on acoustic guitar, and percussionist Larry "Nastyee" Latimer on congas.

But it was the "solo" song "Living for the City" that would find TONTO firing on all circuits (or at least firing on many circuits—it had a *lot* of circuits). It's a 7:22 tour de force with the synth tucked in alongside a Fender Rhodes, a Moog bass, an electric piano, live drums, and a play-within-a-play, Shakespearean in its ambitions and grandeur without the double weddings at the end.

TONTO shows up on two *Fulfillingness' First Finale* tracks, "Creepin'" and "They Won't Go When I Go," both of which contain ample synthetic mood swirls. The former is highlighted by Minnie Riperton's background vocals. The latter, cowritten by

Yvonne Wright, is at turns bold and modest, and certainly stark. It's a classical hymn that Stevie paired with "Never Dreamed You'd Leave in Summer" at Michael Jackson's 2009 funeral. It's among the most striking songs he's written.

Many attribute the bleak, Revelation-invoking "They Won't Go When I Go," in which Stevie leaves the sinners behind, to his August 6, 1973, car accident that left him in a coma for days and out of the public eye for six weeks. As with Dylan's 1966 motorcycle crash, there's an aura of mystery surrounding the accident, with some associates on the outer rim of Stevie's inner circle questioning the severity and others if it actually happened.

What did happen is that Stevie showed up a few weeks after the crash with a scar on his head. And that he joined Elton John onstage at the Boston Garden on September 23, accompanying John on the Rolling Stones' "Honky Tonk Women," a frequent encore song on John's first *Goodbye Yellow Brick Road* tour, and "Superstition," which John played occasionally in 1973.

While there had been cracks developing in the working relationship between Margouleff and Cecil and Stevie, the situation surrounding the accident seems to have precipitated its demise. As recounted by Mark Ribowsky, the duo wasn't allowed access to Stevie after the accident, shut off by an inner circle growing hostile. This dynamic replicated itself in the recording process, culminating with Cecil being upbraided for telling Stevie's friends to be quiet in the studio. Cecil walked out of the studio and never recorded Stevie again. A few months later, Margouleff quit the team.

THE SONG

In addition to the two TONTO songs, *Fulfillingness' First Finale* included two best-selling singles. "You Haven't Done Nothin'" was released August 7, 1974, and it was Stevie's third number-one pop and R&B hit, following "Fingertips" and "Superstition." Propelled by funky-funky clavinet and background vocals from the Jackson 5, the anti-Nixon anthem leans heavily into Stevie's fondness for Sly and the Family Stone's rock-funk. And it's got a drum machine kickin' at the back. Sly was the first artist to hit number one with a drum machine on 1971's super-slim click-track "Family Affair."

The second single, "Boogie on Reggae Woman," stalled at number three on the pop charts, but was the second of four consecutive R&B number ones. The song is all but perfect. As Stevie said in a 1974 *Melody Maker* interview, "You hear 'Boogie on Reggae Woman,' you think of hangin' out somewhere beautiful." And that's because it is beautiful. Stevie sings and plays Fender Rhodes, piano, harmonica, drums, and Moog bass on the track.

Different critics find different strengths in the song. Questionable ethnic reference aside, a 1974 *Village Voice* reviewer claimed that "the real prize here is Stevie's singing. He slurs that word reggae in a way that defies mimicry, as if it comes from some primary source, the groove of the Congolese collective tongue." A *Crawdaddy* reviewer marveled over "his meanest harmonica solo since the old days," and in 1976 a *Black Music* writer used the song as the prime example of the synthesizer sound the "gurgle," "which can remind one of a bass that hasn't been properly plugged in. This can vary from a deep crackle to a demented fuzz screech and can also be made to sound both deep and squeaky, as in Stevie's 'Boogie on Reggae Woman.'"

For Steve Lodder, author of *Stevie Wonder: A Musical Guide to the Classic Albums*, "it's the bassline, and its sound, that's the most startling thing about this track." He later raves, "There isn't really a precedent for this bass part—plenty of synth basslines, but none as relentlessly groovy and busy as this."

Finally, James E. Perone, author of *The Sound of Stevie Wonder: His Words and Music* (2006), claims that "ultimately, 'Boogie on Reggae Woman' is perfectly balanced in every way, as a composition, and as an instrumental and vocal performance and record production." He goes on to say that "it is one of Wonder's greatest achievements."

Me? I like the harmonica. It's his most freewheeling and joyous playing on any recording.

Stevie was rewarded for his vocal efforts on the song with a Best R&B Vocal Performance, Male Grammy in 1975.

MORE ABOUT THAT HARMONICA

Stevie was playing drums and pianos from an incredibly early age and tacked on other instruments along the way, including a Hohner chromatic harmonica he received from a neighbor. During his first audition at Motown, it was the harmonica playing that stood out.

According to Supreme Mary Wilson, "I especially remember him playing a harmonica he'd brought with him. Of course we were all dumbstruck with amazement."

Early on when Motown was trying to figure out what to do with Stevie, they went back and forth on whether he was a musician who could sing or a singer who could play instruments, taking a long while to concede that he was both and more.

His debut single, "I Call It Pretty Music, but the Old People Call It the Blues," featured vocals and harmonica, but his debut album, *The Jazz Soul of Little Stevie* (1962), includes the liner note: "At the present time, Stevie plays the bongos, drums, organs, piano, and the harmonica which he has been playing since he was five, and at which he excels." He played harmonica on five tracks, "Square," "Paulsby," "Some Other Time," "Session Number 112," and "Bam," but didn't sing. It's his only instrumental album aside from 1968's weird *Eivets Rednow*, although over a third of *Stevie Wonder's Journey through "The Secret Life of Plants"* is instrumental.

But on his second album, Motown did a 180. *Tribute to Uncle Ray* (1962), which should include piano playing, instead says, "In this album, Stevie foregoes his playing of the harmonica, piano, organ, drums and bongos in favor of his vocal abilities." "Foregoes" is an interesting choice of verbs.

The third LP famously includes the mostly instrumental chart-topping harmonica romp "Fingertips," and from then on, Stevie songs frequently wed vocals and harmonica, such as *With a Song in My Heart*'s "On the Sunny Side of the Street" (1963) and "Hey Harmonica Man" from the we-have-no-idea-what-we're-doing-with-him LP *Stevie at the Beach* (1964).

After "Fingertips," the harmonica highlight of Stevie's early career is on the cover of Ron Miller and Orlando Murden's "For Once in My Life" (1968). By the classic album period, Stevie had taken a relative step back, although the period includes highlights such as the ambling "Too High" and the iconic melody from "Isn't She Lovely."

There are no authoritative lists of the greatest harmonica players, although *American Songwriter*'s "The 11 Best Harmonica Players Ever" offers a fairly representative sample of what's valued. The list includes Stevie, Little Walter, the second Sonny Boy Williamson, Toots Thielemans, John Popper, and Bob Dylan. Other online lists focus exclusively on blues players and still others less on fame and commercial recognition and more on actual harmonica prowess on the routine diatonic (what Stevie uses on "Boogie on Reggae Woman") and the more difficult chromatic ("Isn't She Lovely") instruments. Many of Stevie's rock contemporaries who played the harmonica, such as Neil Young and Mick Jagger, even J. Geils Band's Magic Dick ("Whammer Jammer"), don't make many of these lists.

Beyond his own recordings, Stevie has played the harmonica on scores of other artists'. His first guest appearance, contemporaneous with his first releases in 1962, was on "Someday Pretty Baby" by Singin' Sammy Ward. He knocks the doors off the studio after being implored to "Blow it, Stevie!"

His most notable harmonica guest appearances include a trio of mid-1980s hits: Elton John's "I Guess That's Why They Call It the Blues," Chaka Khan's "I Feel for You," and Dionne Warwick and Friends' "That's What Friends Are For." You probably thought of the harmonica riff on each of these as you read the titles.

GEEKING OUT ON SONG VERSIONS

A final note on "Boogie on Reggae Woman" and all that wild harmonica playing: the mysterious case of the proliferating versions of the song.

The original 1974 US Tamla single lists the time as 4:05, whereas the UK single doesn't list a time. In a very unscientific observation of online recordings of original US and UK vinyl recordings of the song, the actual single time appears to be 3:58 with the vocals coming in at 0:27. At about 3:12 Stevie yells out "Ho!" leaving a 0:57 fade-out that includes a minor non-lexical vocable (a yell) about ten seconds before the end.

The original 7-inch is the most concise version, as one would expect for a single, although slightly against practice since label times in the era were typically briefer than actual play times to trick DJs into unknowingly playing longer songs.

The "single version" that appears on the 1996 hits collection *Song Review* is listed at 4:09 but clocks in at 4:05. Vocals come in at 0:28. It seems to have an extra second at the beginning and a marginally longer fade-out. This version appears to be a slightly extended version of the original single.

The *Fulfillingness' First Finale* (1974) version is listed at 4:55. Vocals come in at 0:27. Stevie yells "Ho!" at 3:31 and follows that with a "Yeow!" at 3:35. The rest of the song is instrumental fade-out, about 1:20. There is a minor non-lexical vocable about thirty seconds before the end. What this means is that at least part of the vocal track on the LP version is different than the single version, although the instrumental track seems to be the same, but extended for twenty extra seconds here.

The LP version fades out slightly before crossfading with the next song "Creepin'." *The Complete Stevie Wonder* (2005) and *Stevie Wonder's Original Musiquarium I* (1982) include the same version, although the latter leads directly into the new song "That Girl."

The *At the Close of a Century* (1999) version lasts 5:12. It's the same version as the original LP version, but with the "Yeow!" coming with about 1:37 remaining, tacking on about seventeen additional seconds at the end, delivering a major bass Moog, synth, harmonica, and piano jam. It feels ever so slightly slower. The same version is found on 2002's *The Definitive Collection* Deluxe Edition. The 4:11 "Single Version" found on the single-disc *The Definitive Collection* starts about two seconds earlier but appears to be a truncated version of the Deluxe Edition version, not a version of the original single.

The *Number Ones* (2007) version is listed at 4:47. The vocals come in at 0:27. Stevie yells "Ho!" and 3:15 and there's no "Yeow!" leaving a 1:32 fade-out. There is the non-lexical vocable about forty-five seconds before the end. So, this seems to be the original single vocals mixed with the LP version of the track that has a longer fade-out.

The *Additional Singles and Rarities* (2019) version is 4:50. It starts earlier than the other versions with a unique count-off and vocals beginning at 0:36, tacking on about nine seconds at the beginning. Stevie yells "Ho!" at 3:19, without a "Yeow!" leaving a 1:30 fadeout and a grouping with the single version.

So what does this all mean, aside from the fact that Motown quality control seems to be all over the place?

First, there seems to be different vocal tracks, or at least different vocal edits, for the single version (no "Yeow!") and the album versions (includes "Yeow!"). The yell near the end of the song must be on the instrumental track since it's on all versions.

Second, the instrumental track for all versions seems to be the same, it just starts and stops at different places. The *Additional Singles and Rarities* version has the earliest start, at a count-off, and the *At the Close of a Century/Number Ones* version goes on the longest. If the two version were combined, the full song would run 5:21 as released, although it's unclear how long the song goes on after the fade.

All of this time and length minutiae is a long way of saying that while it's laudable that Motown has released *The Complete Stevie Wonder*, *Additional Singles and Rarities*, *Mono Singles* (which stops in 1971), and *Remixes* (which starts in 1978), more attention needs to be paid to individual albums and/or thematic collections. Maybe there isn't the rare material (or audience demand?) to warrant these releases, but if there is, Polydor's work with James Brown is a super-bad reference point.

Chapter Six Playlist

"Girl Blue," Stevie Wonder

"You've Got It Bad Girl," Stevie Wonder

"Blame It on the Sun," Stevie Wonder

"He's Misstra Know-It-All," Stevie Wonder

"They Won't Go When I Go," Stevie Wonder

"Honky Tonk Women," Elton John

"Family Affair," Sly and the Family Stone

"Whammer Jammer," J. Geils Band

"Someday Pretty Baby," Singin' Sammy Ward

"Boogie on Reggae Woman" (single version), Stevie Wonder

"Boogie on Reggae Woman" (LP version), Stevie Wonder

7

"HAPPY BIRTHDAY"

Social Justice

Stevie Wonder's career has been bolstered by his tireless commitment to social and racial justice. He's lent his name, his songs, and his time to causes including Ethiopian famine, the observation of a Martin Luther King Jr. holiday, and the wrongful incarceration of boxer Rubin "Hurricane" Carter. For these actions and his music work, he's been richly rewarded with honors around the world.

This chapter takes a look at some of Stevie's activism and charitable contributions to society, zooming in on the social impact of "Happy Birthday," the 1981 single from 1980's *Hotter Than July* that contributed to the establishment of the Martin Luther King Jr. holiday.

THE BACKSTORY, OR HOW WE JUMP FROM 1974 TO 1981

Fulfillingness' First Finale was released July 22, 1974. *Songs in the Key of Life* was released twenty-six months later on September 28, 1976. This was a lifetime in Motown Years.

Stevie launched a full-scale US tour for *Fulfillingness' First Finale* in the second half of 1974, continuing into Japan and Canada in spring 1975. But by summer 1975, the wait for new material was a running concern for Motown, which had already sold the album to distributors. Stevie wore a T-shirt declaring "We're Almost Finished!" and Motown personnel wore similar "Stevie's Nearly Ready" tops.

Around the same time, Stevie also said he was sick of the United States post-Nixon, so he would retire from music and move to Ghana to work with children. He made a similar claim in 2021. The Ghana threat gave Motown the heebie-jeebies, and, despite no discernable progress on a new album, on August 5, 1975, Wonder re-signed with Motown for the largest contract to that time, $37 million for seven years and seven albums.

Being shown the money seemed to give Stevie the encouragement to pull the long-awaited project together, ever so slightly. On September 7, 1975, Stevie invited friends and press to Long View Farm in North Brookfield, Massachusetts, to hear tracks from the new album.

Still, nothing very public happened for most of 1976 until the September *Songs in the Key of LIfe* release, which was followed in December by the first single, "I Wish," and in March 1977 by "Sir Duke." All three discs went to number one of the pop and R&B charts, and in February 1977 he cleaned up at the Grammys: Album of the Year, Producer of the Year, Best Male Pop Vocal Performance, and Best Male R&B Vocal Performance (for "I Wish"). The double

LP contained seventeen songs plus the four-song *A Something's Extra* EP. It now shows up on many "best albums of all time" lists.

While this would have been the perfect time to tour *Songs in the Key of Life* and consolidate his place at the top of the recording and performance pyramid, Stevie instead moved further from the public eye, only making a handful of appearances, mainly at awards shows, in 1977 and 1978. He wouldn't tour *Songs in the Key of Life* until 2014.

Capitalizing on *Songs in the Key of Life*'s commercial success, Motown released the forty-song triple LP *Looking Back* for the 1977 holiday season. The set covers Stevie's career through *Where I'm Coming From*. Motown had wanted to sell the set in 1974, but Stevie said no. It's a well-curated collection and includes the first release of Wonder's co-penned 1967 version of Aretha Franklin's 1973 number-one R&B smash "Until You Come Back to Me (That's What I'm Gonna Do)."

Stevie headlined the 50th Birthday Benefit Concert for Dr. King on January 15, 1979, at the Atlanta Omni Arena. The show was a benefit for the Martin Luther King Center for Social Change. The next month saw him recording in earnest again for his next project, the experimental soundtrack LP *Stevie Wonder's Journey through "The Secret Life of Plants."* The double LP was released on October 30, 1979, and was followed by a late-fall eight-city tour. The shows included a performance of the LP followed by a set of greatest hits.

Returning to earlier work patterns, the turnaround time for 1980's *Hotter Than July* was less than a year, released September 29. The album was critically well received, but it was clear that Stevie was no longer trailblazing musical paths and instead starting to follow those ruts in the road, in particular disco ("All I Do," a take on his unreleased 1966 co-composition "All I Do Is Think about You") and country ("I Ain't Gonna Stand for It").

Unlike the previous two albums, Stevie took to the road for an extended period to support *Hotter Than July*. After a warm-up date August 24 at the Roxy in Los Angeles, his first club date in eight years, Stevie played an early September week of "Hotter Than July Music Picnic" shows at London's Wembley Arena. At the final show, September 7, Stevie was joined by Diana Ross and Marvin Gaye on their recent single "Pops, We Love You." Wonder would spend late October through late January 1981 on and off the road in the United States and Canada before extending the tour to the Far East and Europe through June 1, 1981.

Half of the LP's ten songs were released as singles in the United States or UK, with the lead 7-inch "Master Blaster (Jammin')," Stevie's deepest dive into reggae, reaching number five on the pop charts and number one on the R&B (soul) chart. But it was the fourth UK single, "Happy Birthday," that made the biggest impact on American history. It's jaunty synth pop that wouldn't be totally out of place in the catalog of contemporaneous New Romantics such as Human League ("[Keep Feeling] Fascination").

THE SONG

Stevie met MLK in 1966 at a Southern Christian Leadership Conference event at Soldier Field during the Chicago Freedom

Movement, an effort that increased Black activism in northern cities and, in part, led to the Fair Housing Act.

Soon after MLK was assassinated on April 4, 1968, John Conyers, a Black Michigan Democratic representative, and Edward Brooke, a Black Republican from Massachusetts, wrote a bill seeking to declare Martin Luther King Jr.'s birthday, January 15, a US national holiday. The bipartisan bill finally came before the US House in 1979 and was defeated by five votes.

Stevie spoke and played "My Cherie Amour" at Representative Conyers's funeral at the Greater Grace Temple in Detroit on November 4, 2019. Brooke was the first Black US senator elected by voters. He died in 2015 and, thankfully, John Kerry didn't sing at his funeral.

After the failed vote, Stevie went into overdrive. Working with King's widow Coretta Scott King and backed by the power of "Happy Birthday," he assembled the Rally for Peace on January 15, 1981, at the Washington Monument. The event, which included appearances by Diana Ross, Gladys Knight, Jesse Jackson, and Gil Scott-Heron, attracted about fifty thousand people and kicked off a publicity and petition-signing campaign in support of the holiday. The petition garnered over six million signatures, the largest such collection in US history.

Indiana representative Katie Hall reintroduced MLK holiday legislation in July 1983. The bill passed both Chambers of Congress with north of 75 percent of the vote, and President Ronald Reagan signed it into law on November 2, 1983. Set by law on the third Monday in January, the first MLK Day was federally celebrated on January 20, 1986. Not all states celebrated the holiday until January 2000, when New Hampshire became the last state to name a holiday after King.

Stevie participated in a live NBC broadcast from the John F. Kennedy Center for the Performing Arts in Washington, DC, on January 20, 1986, to celebrate the first holiday. The night included appearances by dozens of stars, including Diana Ross, Lionel Richie, Whitney Houston, Eddie Murphy, and Elizabeth Taylor. Bob Dylan performed "I Shall Be Released," then was joined by Stevie and Peter, Paul and Mary on a rough version of "Blowin' in the Wind." The night ended with an extended "Happy Birthday" finale.

Proceeds from the Washington concert went to the King Center for Nonviolent Social Change.

While there is a long history of protest songs used to publicize injustices and to unite and form oppositional communities, "Happy Birthday" seems to be a unique case of a direct link between a song and US national legislation. Although, truth be told, "Happy Birthday" isn't as much a protest song as a political intervention or an awareness anthem.

Multiple sources credit Stevie's early interest in politics to his teacher/mentor Ted Hull, who started working with him in 1963. While Wonder was obviously no stranger to racial oppression growing up in America in the 1950s and 1960s, his close relationship with an older white man afforded him a different perspective on local, national, and international issues as they traveled together around the country and the world.

Although Wonder had been to the Nixon White House in late 1969 to receive the Distinguished Service Award, two of his major protest songs were anti-Nixon tunes. Both "Big Brother," almost *Talking Book*'s first single, and the number one "You Haven't Done Nothin'" take Nixon to task for calling out Black people without offering any help.

Beyond these Tricky Dick raspberries, Stevie's mid-1970s protest more generally took aim at the exploitation and plight of the Black poor in America. The lead track in this category is the epic "Living for the City," followed by the *Songs in the Key of Life* trio "Village Ghetto Land," "Pastime Paradise," and "Black Man." 1987's *Characters*' song "Dark 'n' Lovely" would take a more global perspective on similar themes. And, more directly, 1982's "Front Line" from *Stevie Wonder's Original Musiquarium I* tackled the plight of Vietnam vets, and "It's Wrong (Apartheid)" from 1985's *In Square Circle* tackled, well, you can guess.

Beyond "Happy Birthday," Stevie's greatest contribution to positive social change has been through contributing his time, money, presence, and performances. This propensity appears to have kicked off on August 23, 1963. Stevie took part in the Benefit for the Negro American Labor Council at the Apollo Theater to raise money for unemployed workers to travel to the August 28 March on Washington. Stevie helped to raise $30,000 alongside activist actors Sidney Poitier, Paul Newman, and Joanne Woodward, and performers such as Tony Bennett, Thelonious Monk, Art Blakey and the Jazz Messengers, and Quincy Jones.

Five years later, on May 9, 1968, Stevie took part in the Southern Christian Leadership Conference's Poor People's Campaign benefit concert at the Atlanta Civic Center. The event was organized by Berry Gordy and featured Motown acts including Diana Ross and the Supremes, the Temptations, and Gladys Knight & the Pips. There's an impossibly small clip of Stevie performing in glorious color in a brief online documentary about the event.

On December 10, 1972, Stevie took part in the John Sinclair Freedom Rally in Ann Arbor, Michigan, aka the Ten for Two concert (also the name of the concert documentary film). John Sinclair was the manager of Detroit punks the MC5 and a member of the White Panthers, a white group that supported the goals of the Black Panthers. Under draconian Michigan laws, Sinclair was given a ten-year prison sentence for possession of two marijuana joints. The concert was intended to get him freed from prison, which inadvertently worked when the state legislature changed the laws and he was freed a few days after the show.

The highlight of the event for many attendees was seeing John Lennon live onstage. This was mitigated by the four songs he and Yoko Ono played that evening, all from 1972's aggressively unlistenable *Some Time in New York City*. To make matters worse, Lennon brought along Lower Manhattan pal David Peel and his music-averse protest froth.

Stevie marveled with an opening "For Once in My Life," a long, trippy cover of Sly Stone's "Somebody's Watching You," from

1969's *Stand!*, dedicated to all the undercover cops in the audience, and "Heaven Help Us All."

On May 20, 1972, Wonder performed at "The Concert for the Blood" at West Point's Michie Stadium to raise funds for sickle cell anemia research. A clip of "For Once in My Life" is available online. The concert was organized by the military academy's Contemporary Affairs Seminar, part of a rising Black movement on campus following Nixon's 1971 order to put a Confederate memorial on the Hudson River campus.

A year later, on April 25, 1973, Stevie joined Ray Charles and Al Hibbler at the Philharmonic Hall in New York City for An Out-of-Sight Night. The event was designed to benefit Choose, Inc., a nonprofit that tried to better integrate the blind into everyday life. Hibbler was a vocalist for Duke Ellington's Orchestra in the late 1940s. His biggest hit with Sir Duke was 1944's "Do Nothin' till You Hear from Me," which hit the top of the Black charts for eight weeks. Hibbler had a long solo career, highlighted by his 1955 R&B number one of "Unchained Melody," a song most famously captured by the Righteous Brothers that's been covered well over six hundred times, hitting the charts more than a dozen times.

Later that year, on August 6, Wonder had his South Carolina car accident that put him out of commission for many weeks. His first date back was a November 10, 1973, benefit show at Shaw University in Raleigh, North Carolina. He was a trustee of the school, which was the first historically Black university in the South, created December 1, 1865, less than eight months after the end of the Civil War.

Stevie was on the Shaw bill with Labelle, the vocal group fronted by Patti LaBelle. That same year Stevie wrote and coproduced, with group manager Vicki Wickham, "Open Up Your Heart," a non-charting single from their *Pressure Cookin'* LP. Wonder has been a lifelong friend of Patti LaBelle, and the two were featured at the September 24, 2016, dedication ceremony for the National Museum of African American History and Culture. Stevie performed "Where Is Our Love Song," which he eventually released as a 2020 single featuring Gary Clark Jr.

The now-gone Houston Astrodome hosted Night of the Hurricane II on January 25, 1976. It was a follow-up to the wildly successful Night of the Hurricane at Madison Square Garden in December 1975, an event designed to support boxer Rubin "Hurricane" Carter, wrongly jailed as a result of racial profiling. Bob Dylan had headlined the first Night of the Hurricane in December 1975, his song "Hurricane" contributing to Carter's status as a cause célèbre. Dylan and his Rolling Thunder Revue, playing a three-hour headlining set, were preceded onstage by local bands, main opening act Wonder, and MC Isaac Hayes. Backed by Wonderlove, Stevie played an hour-plus set that included mid-seventies hits, the yet-to-be released "Contusion," and the O'Jays' "I Love Music."

Stevie headlined his next major benefit show, an August 24, 1980, show at Los Angeles' Roxy Theatre that doubled as a warm-up for UK *Hotter Than July* shows. The show was designed to help the children of Eula Love, a woman who had been gunned down by the LA police in January 1979. The generous setlist included the debut of the future concert stalwart "Ribbon in the Sky" and the beautiful 1940s-standard-sounding unreleased track "Reflections of You."

Wonder once again shared the stage with Dylan at the June 6, 1982, Peace Sunday Committee Benefit show at the Rose Bowl in Pasadena, California. Echoing King's "I Have a Dream," the slogan for this anti–nuclear arms show was "We Have a Dream." Other performers included Gil Scott-Heron, Joan Baez, Stevie Nicks, and Tom Petty and the Heartbreakers. Eighty-five thousand fans got to hear Wonder serve up a trio of recent hits, "Front Line," "Master Blaster (Jammin')," "Do I Do," and a "We Demand World Peace Today" chant.

With Nelson Mandela two years away from his release from prison and six years from his election as South Africa's president, his seventieth birthday was celebrated a few weeks early with a tribute concert at London's Wembley Stadium on June 11, 1988. It was rough going. It took a while to convince Stevie to join the show. He committed only a few days before, accepting an opening that was reserved for a Prince and Bono duet (which wouldn't happen until 1995, when the pair performed "The Cross" at a Prince after-show in Dublin). When it came time for Stevie's set, his Synclavier hard drive was missing, and he refused to go on. Tracy Chapman performed her second set of the day, including "Fast Car," which in 2023 would make her the first Black woman songwriter to top the country charts, courtesy of Luke Combs's cover. Stevie eventually was coaxed onto the stage and performed a short set.

March 5, 1989, saw Stevie raising $350,000 for Concern Foundation's Minnie Riperton Fund, which focuses on supporting breast cancer research. He played to a sold-out Universal Amphitheatre in Universal City, California.

After this point, Stevie regularly participated in countless benefit and charity events, but, like the Peace Sunday concert, these events are often less localized and more functions of national and global concerns. These include events such as the September 21, 2001, America: A Tribute to Heroes concert to raise funds for victims and families of the 9/11 terrorist attacks; the January 15, 2005, "A Concert for Hope" Tsunami Relief Telethon; and the April 18, One World: Together at Home 2020 telecast to raise funds for the World Health Organization and frontline workers battling COVID-19.

But perhaps the benefit closest to Stevie's heart is his House Full of Toys concert, which started in 1991 and has been running more or less yearly since 2000. The shows benefit children, people with disabilities, and families in need, occasionally focusing on specific groups, such as victims of California wildfires, the beneficiaries of the 2018 show. Beyond the charity, these shows can be special occasions. At the 2017 show, Stevie performed all of *Talking Book* and *Innervisions*, and he typically pulls out some holiday rarities. It's what Christmas means to him.

Chapter Seven Playlist

"Pops, We Love You," Diana Ross, Marvin Gaye, Smokey Robinson, and Stevie Wonder

"(Keep Feeling) Fascination," The Human League

"I Shall Be Released," Bob Dylan

"Dark 'n' Lovely," Stevie Wonder

"It's Wrong (Apartheid)," Stevie Wonder

"Somebody's Watching You," Sly and the Family Stone

"Do Nothin' till You Hear from Me," Duke Ellington

"Unchained Melody," Al Hibbler

"Open Up Your Heart," Labelle

"Hurricane," Bob Dylan

"Fast Car," Tracy Chapman

8

"I JUST CALLED TO SAY I LOVE YOU"

Midlife Crisis

The 1980s served as a turning point for many musicians whose first success arrived in the 1960s. For some, it was simply giving up on musical dignity, such as Jefferson Airplane, countercultural heroes of the 1960s and, as Jefferson Starship and then Starship, sellout villains of the 1980s with "We Built This City." Others, such as the Rolling Stones with *Dirty Work*, would hit rock bottom before leveling out to a lucrative career of recorded mediocrity. For others, such as Neil Young (*Landing on Water*), Bob Dylan (*Down in the Groove*), and Paul Simon (*Hearts and Bones*), 1980s failures flushed the system of unwanted waste and opened the pipes to a flow of, if not genius work, at least respectable production. (I promise that's the last plumbing metaphor I'll use.)

Mixed in with inevitable aging was an evolving music indus-try. The major labels were stymied by an economic recession in the early part of the decade. Record sales suffered, and many of the extravagances afforded artists in the mid- and late 1970s were off the table, including unlimited studio time. Around the same time, digital technology began to change not only how music was recorded but also how it sounded and how it was distributed. As a blanket statement, I'd say that the technology made it easier for artists to record music, which also made it easier to record bad music. And, when the proliferation of compact discs demanded seventy-seven-minute LPs, artists were compelled to cram all that bad music into every release. But that's another book.

Stevie started his career young, and his midlife crisis artistic period also hit young, in his mid-thirties. When he was thirty-four, he would release his best-selling single of all time, "I Just Called to Say I Love You." The single is also his most critically berated song, a "We Built This City" that marks the beginning of the second half of and more or less portends a post–*Dirty Work* career.

THE BACKSTORY

The five-year period between the September 1980 release of *Hotter Than July* and the September 1985 release of *In Square Circle* would prove to be unpredictable, simultaneously artistically sparse and commercially bountiful.

Just as *Songs in the Key of Life* was soon followed by the early greatest hits collection *Looking Back*, *Hotter Than July* was followed in May 1982 by *Stevie Wonder's Original Musiquarium I*. The double-LP collection of later greatest hits features major singles, from *Music of My Mind*'s "Superwoman (Where Were You When I

Needed You)" through "Master Blaster (Jammin')," and adds four new songs/singles. And, following *Fulfillingness' First Finale*, it's the second Stevie LP with a title word that spellcheck seriously dislikes.

According to Ribowsky, Stevie was approaching bankruptcy just as his personal profligacies of the 1970 recording industry met the recession, and he negotiated a $3 million payout to release the album with four new songs. The double-disc fulfilled his most recent obligations to Motown, and he promptly signed another seven-year contract.

The collection followed the December 1981 release of the "That Girl" single. At best, the song can be described as slight, unchallenging R&B, the type of song I might put on while washing the dishes and then minutes later think that I should put on some music while I do the dishes. It also spent nine weeks at number one of the R&B charts, the longest stretch at number one of Stevie's career, and was the top R&B single of 1982 (noting that the chart actually changed from Hot Soul Singles to Black Singles in 1982). The song beat out Marvin Gaye's vastly superior "Sexual Healing," which spent eight weeks on top at the end of the year.

"That Girl" was followed by the enjoyable post-disco jam "Do I Do." The edited (5:30) single hit number two on the Black Singles chart, but the keeper is the 10:30 LP version, which includes an extended solo from jazz trumpeter Dizzy Gillespie and Stevie offering a silly take on "Rapper's Delight." In a career of studio polish, it's one of the few times when it feels like the tape's rolling and everyone's having some fun.

But the highlight of the rollicking tune is Nathan East's brisk and precise bass line. And it's one that I'd swear the Smiths lifted for "Barbarism Begins at Home," the epic track from their 1985 LP *Meat Is Murder*. While the late Smiths bassist Andy Rourke doesn't seem to have discussed that particular track, he did admit in a 2017 interview that if he could only listen to one bassline for the rest of his life, it would be James Jamerson's "I Was Made to Love Her" riff.

The ballad "Ribbon in the Sky" was released in June 1982, and it hit number 10 on the Black Singles chart. It's been a mainstay of Stevie's live show, and he played it at Whitney Houston's funeral on February 18, 2012.

The final single, "Front Line," released in 1983, might be the last super-funk Stevie song. Some might even say it's the last great Stevie song, although Ribowsky pegs that at "I Wish." "Front Line" is a story-song like "Living for the City" about a life that got away after volunteering for Vietnam. The single failed to chart. Stevie played the song live a handful of times, most notably at the Vietnam Veterans Benefit 1986 on February 24 at the Forum in Los Angeles, a show co-headlined by Neil Young, and the Welcome Home 1987 concert in Landover, Maryland, a benefit concert for Vietnam veterans that also included James Brown on the bill.

These singles mark the coda of Wonder's most creative and critically acclaimed period. And just as he was at a crossroads in the mid-1970s, he didn't seem to have a clear path forward at this time—the well seemed to have dried up, and he wouldn't release any of his own new material until "I Just Called to Say I Love You" on August 1, 1984.

But he did famously release work with other artists during this time, including major hits with Paul McCartney, Elton John, and Chaka Khan. More on this in later chapters.

Live, he hoed an odd row during this half decade. The *Hotter Than July* tour ended on June 1, 1981, at the Palais des Sports in Grenoble, France, the American student study-abroad mecca. His 1982 live shows didn't kick into high gear until the June 6 Peace Sunday show, which was followed by dates throughout the summer US stadium tour Budweiser Superfest, along with Quincy Jones, Aretha Franklin, and Ashford & Simpson, and a string of fall shows in Japan. Stevie would later feature in a "Superstition"-driven Bud Light commercial that aired during the 2013 Super Bowl.

He followed in 1983 with a baffling schedule. He appeared at the Motown 25: Yesterday, Today, Forever concert on March 25 at the Pasadena Civic Auditorium. The show was broadcast on May 16 on NBC, and the world broke: Michael Jackson introduced his moonwalk during "Billie Jean." The next day there were girls at my high school acting in ways I'd never seen anyone act. It was truly astonishing.

A week before the 1983 Motown 25 broadcast, Stevie appeared on NBC's *Saturday Night Live*. He performed "Go Home" and "Overjoyed," neither of which would be released until two and a half years later on 1985's *In Square Circle*. Motown had hoped to fast-track the LP release, but Stevie was sidetracked by a soundtrack request from Dionne Warwick.

After a trio of shows in Canada at the end of the summer, he took up short-term fall residencies on the "You and Me" tour at theaters in/near Boston, New York, Miami, Philadelphia, and San Francisco.

In April 1984 he performed a string of "Comes Home to Detroit" dates at the Masonic Temple Theatre. An hour of one show was broadcast on June 8, 1984, on Showtime as *Stevie Wonder Comes Home*. The complete two-hour, twenty-minute show from April 14 can be found online. It's energetic and engaging and features such original rarities as "It's Growing" and "Nobody Loves Me," a version of the cowritten "I Can't Help It" that he gave to Michael Jackson for *Off the Wall*, and a cover of Ernest Tubb's "Walking the Floor Over You." Stevie's live studio version of the Jackson song also circulates online, and it's a crime it hasn't been officially released.

Following Detroit, Stevie was on the road in Europe from early June through early September 1984, by which time "I Just Called to Say I Love" you had exploded.

THE SONG

"I Just Called to Say I Love You" was released on September 1, 1984, with an instrumental version on the B-side; both versions are 4:16. It was the lead single from the soundtrack to the Gene Wilder vehicle *The Woman in Red* (not to be confused with Chris de Burgh's "The Lady in Red"). The album version runs 6:16, with a long, painful vocoder section that's edited from the single version. The single replaced the album version on some later editions of LP. A Europe-only maxi-single includes a an extended 6:44 version backed with a 5:03 instrumental version, both of which seem to have eluded *The Complete Stevie Wonder* compilers.

Damn, the song was popular. "I Just Called to Say I Love You" topped pretty much every chart worldwide. It's Stevie's best-selling US single and the best-selling Motown single in the UK, where it was also Stevie's only number one. It's been featured in dozens of TV shows and was the soundtrack for a 1986 Sprint TV commercial, reportedly upping the telecom's business by 25 percent within three days.

Wonder performed the song on *The Cosby Show* episode "A Touch of Wonder," which aired on NBC on February 20, 1986. He was accompanied by cast members Phylicia Rashad, Lisa Bonet, Malcolm-Jamal Warner, Tempestt Bledsoe, and Keshia Knight Pulliam.

It won a Golden Globe for Best Original Song, which is a songwriting award. It beat out "Against All Odds (Take a Look at Me Now)" by Phil Collins, "Footloose" by Kenny Loggins and Dean Pitchford, "Ghostbusters" by Ray Parker Jr., "No More Lonely Nights" by pal Paul McCartney, and "When Doves Cry" by Prince. And it bumped Prince's "Let's Go Crazy" from the top of the pop charts.

The song also won an Academy Award for Best Original Song, beating out Collins, Loggins, Parker, and Dean Pitchford and Tom

Snow for "Let's Hear It for the Boy" from *Footloose*. Wonder dedicated the Oscar to Nelson Mandela, and the next day his music was banned in South Africa.

So why do so many people hate "I Just Called to Say I Love You"?

Biographer Ribowsky calls it a "sheer pop fluff ballad" and "the kind of commercial contrivance Stevie has pardoned with 'Ebony and Ivory,' and upon initial listening just as bad." But he admits that it has a "catchy soundscape."

In *Stevie Wonder: A Musical Guide to the Classic Albums*, which takes an "unashamedly musicianly" approach, Steve Loder offers three long paragraphs about what's wrong with the song. It's all interesting and worth sharing (and accurate), but well beyond the scope of reproduction here due to copyright limitations. But some highlights include observations that "the rhythm track is plodding," "there's not a tiny spark of creative energy on display," and it's "like a box of soggy fireworks." This is followed by the extended observation about "the lacklustre chordal arrangement, the annoying synth doubling of the tune, the devoid-of-imagination bassline, the predictability of the harmonic moves, the dire change of key in a desperate attempt to inject some life into a track that's going nowhere." Tell us what you really think.

Ultimately for Loder, it's not just the musical depravity on display but the distance between the subtle, intelligent, and curious music of Wonder's past and his "being eaten by pop" in the present.

You need to fall from a great height to sink so low, which is a common thread of 1980s midlife crisis artists.

Alternately, James E. Perone, in *The Sound of Stevie Wonder: His Words and Music*, thinks that "the song and Wonder's recording of it succeed . . . on a certain artistic level." His basic argument is that Wonder has created "totally generic" song, claiming "the brilliance of the recording is in the total focus on simplicity and on the solitary humanity of Stevie Wonder's lead vocal." This is, at least, a generous reading.

A less generous reading of the song was offered by songwriters Lloyd Chiate, who cowrote some Eddie Money songs in the mind-1970s, and Lee Garrett, who wrote or cowrote hundreds of songs, including "Signed, Sealed, Delivered I'm Yours." The duo sued Wonder in October 1985, claiming they wrote the song and he stole it from them after he played it for them. Garrett dropped out of the suit in 1986. Chiate lost the case in 1990 and an appeal in 1992.

Given how much the song has been disliked, it's not surprising that it ended up in court. In testimony, Stevie claimed he wrote the chorus on July 16, 1976. He also said, "I imagined in my mind when hearing the chords that the Beatles were singing with me. And that idea and feeling is what inspired me to use the vocoder, when I heard about the vocoder. And I always imagined myself and the Beatles singing that." I guess creative geniuses work differently than us mortals, but I don't make the jump from this song to the vocoder to the Beatles.

The song's lack of street cred features in the 2000 Stephen Frears film *High Fidelity*. The movie's protagonist owns a hipster Chicago record store that employs music elitist Barry, played by Jack Black. In one scene, a middle-aged guy enters the store and asks if he can have "I Just Called to Say I Love You" for his daughter. Barry says no, and the guy asks why: "Well, it's sentimental tacky crap, that's why not. Do we look like the kind of store that sells 'I Just Called to Say I Love You'? Go to the mall." Prodded, Barry ends up asking if the guy's daughter is in a coma. By the end of the scene, Barry is asking the store for a list of "top five musical crimes perpetrated by Stevie Wonder in the eighties and nineties."

In the film's last moments, Barry goes even further anti-Stevie, wowing everyone with a performance of Marvin's Gaye's "Let's Get It On."

And with that, it's probably the case that, in spite of vitriol directed at "I Just Called to Say I Love You," it's probably not the most hated Stevie song of the 1980s. That honor would go to his duet with Paul McCartney, "Ebony and Ivory," although Stevie tends to shoulder less than half the blame.

"Ebony and Ivory" was released March 29, 1982, the lead single from McCartney's third solo album and eleventh post-Beatles studio LP, *Tug of War*. The McCartney-penned tune was number one on the US pop charts for seven weeks, for Macca trailing only "Hey Jude," which spent nine weeks on top. The album, which topped the US and UK charts, featured another duet with Stevie, "What's

That You're Doing?" This extended track echoing "Do I Do" funks up the electronic experimentations of the previous LP *McCartney II*.

In contrast, "Ebony and Ivory" is anything but funky, and aggressively so. The music has been called "saccharine," but that doesn't go far enough. It's offensive in its soft, rounded synthesizer tones that are obviously intended not to offend even the most sensitive of ears. It's music designed for unsophisticated toddlers. But it's also the more complexly crafted element of the recording.

The lyrics, playing on the similarities and differences between the black and white keys of a piano, oversimplify complicated issues to the point of inanity. And, according to Perrone, it's executed poorly, commenting on "the awkward phrasing of some of the lines in the lyrics and the naivete of the sentiments." All around, it might be the most unsubtle song ever.

As with "I Just Called to Say I Love You," the critical anger toward the song exists in part because of the distance between the quality and intention of McCartney's past work and this endeavor. This is compounded by the inclusion of Wonder. Capturing this sentiment in an online article "Ear Poison Tasting Class: Analyzing Blender's 50 Worst Songs Ever," writer Dan MacCrae says, "This is like Batman and Superman coming together to do something and the end product is the invention of the salmon M&M."

"Ebony and Ivory" is number 10 on *Blender*'s 2020 ranking. It hangs in the same territory with such songs as "Don't Worry, Be Happy" by Bobby McFerrin and "Kokomo" by the Beach Boys, with the vapidity of both pieces almost lessening any harsh evaluation of the McCartney/Wonder duet. The number-one spot goes to Starship's 1985 opus "We Built This City," and I have no quarrel there.

While no other Wonder work ends up on the list, McCartney's 1968 Beatles tune "Ob-La-Di, Ob-La-Da," appears at number 48, in part for its fake Caribbean vibe and also for sentiments that Paul ripped the title off from session conga player Jimmy Smith (who was in Stevie's backing band on his 1965 UK tour). At least "Ebony and Ivory" was an authentic Caribbean song, recorded at producer George Martin's Montserrat studio.

Paul McCartney and Stevie Wonder did in fact perform "Ebony and Ivory" together live—for the first time in 1989 in Inglewood, California, then again at the White House in 2010. No word on whether Barack Obama gave Wonder and McCartney a presidential pardon for the song.

Chapter Eight Playlist

"We Built This City," Starship
"That Girl," Stevie Wonder
"Barbarism Begins at Home," The Smiths
"Front Line," Stevie Wonder
"Walking the Floor Over You," Ernest Tubb
"I Can't Help It," Michael Jackson

"Ebony and Ivory," Paul McCartney and Stevie Wonder

"What's That You're Doing?" Paul McCartney and Stevie Wonder

"Don't Worry, Be Happy," Bobby McFerrin

"Kokomo," The Beach Boys

"Ob-La-Di, Ob-La-Da," The Beatles

9

"FUN DAY"

Soundtracks

This is stating the obvious, but Stevie Wonder is blind. Thus, it might be considered ironic that so much of his work, from television and film appearances to the creation of three complete movie soundtracks and countless music videos, has taken place in visual media. Even his album covers—he's never seen them.

This chapter takes a closer look at Stevie's three soundtrack albums and additional soundtrack work. Of course, the biggest soundtrack song, "I Just Called to Say I Love You," was just covered. As such, with the 1991 *Jungle Fever* song "Fun Day" we'll get less of a focus and more of a fulcrum for the chapter.

STEVIE WONDER'S JOURNEY THROUGH "THE SECRET LIFE OF PLANTS"

The double LP *Stevie Wonder's Journey through "The Secret Life of Plants"* was released October 30, 1979. The music accompanies the

1979 documentary film *Journey through the Secret Life of Plants*, which was adapted from the controversial 1973 book *The Secret Life of Plants* (later titled *A Fascinating Account of the Physical, Emotional and Spiritual Relations Between Plants and Man*). The Harper & Row book was written by Peter Tompkins and Christopher Bird, the ninety-seven-minute film directed by Walon Green.

The book investigates plant sentience (they gave a plant a lie-detector test) and the ability of plants to communicate with humans. It was derided at the time as hippie, proto–New Age pseudoscience akin to fiction, with one critic calling it "the funniest unintentionally funny book of the year." What better way to attract an audience? While no positive evidence has been offered for human-plant communication (aside from me talking to my aloe vera), there is evidence that trees do communicate with one another via their roots in a "mycorrhizal network," or, more colloquially, a Wood Wide Web.

Authors Tompkins and Bird are, at best, suspect in their scientific leanings. Tompkins trucked in books revealing the "secrets" of the Mexican and Great Pyramids, the Bermuda Triangle, and obelisks, a harbinger of a late 1970s conspiracy culture that sent videographers up mountains looking for Noah's Ark and provided Leonard Nimoy a steady paycheck going *In Search of . . .* mummy's curses, bigfoot, and UFO captives. Christopher Bird later wrote the popular tome *The Divining Hand: The 500-Year-Old Mystery of Dowsing*. When you believe in things you don't understand . . .

For all this, the film was brought together by somewhat legitimate players. According to sources, Stevie had been approached to score the film by producer Michael Braun as far back as 1974 during the recording of *Songs in the Key of Life*. Braun had worked in the film industry as an assistant to directors such as Stanley Kubrick and Roman Polanski and, most famously, in 1964 published *Love Me Do! The Beatles Progress*, which John Lennon considered the most honest portrayal of the band's first few years. Braun died in 1997 while producing the *Titanic* stage production.

Braun turned to Walon Green to direct. Green was a successful screenwriter who had been nominated for an Oscar for cowriting *The Wild Bunch* (1969) with director Sam Peckinpah. He won an Academy Award for Best Documentary Feature and a BAFTA Award for Best Documentary in 1973 for *The Hellstrom Chronicle*. The "documentary" pits collective insects versus individualistic humans in a metaphoric battle for the planet. A short pivot to plants and humans.

While creating the score, Wonder worked with a four-track tape that included Braun describing the visuals on one track, engineer Gary Olazabal providing human click-track timing for shots on the second track, and the film's soundtrack (narration, dialogue, etc.) on a third track, leaving him with one track to mix down his musical contributions.

This human relay system wasn't the only unique aspect of recording the score, as Wonder was also a trailblazer in the use of digital technology for this recording. Sony had released the

Sony PCM-1 home digital recorder in September 1977. Stevie supposedly owns two of the prototype machines. For the *Secret Life of Plants*, Stevie took a deep dive into digital technology, not only using the Sony PCM 1600 digital recorder, introduced to the commercial market in 1978, but also Harry Mendell's Computer Music Melodian, which can make any sound into a musical sound. Mendell would receive sound designer credits for the next few albums.

There is an array of "firsts" in digital recording history that stretch back to 1971 when Steve Marcus and Jiro Inagaki & Soul Media released the direct-to-digital LP *Something* in Japan. The album includes two slow versions of the George Harrison Beatles classic. Stevie wasn't the first to market with a digitally recorded major-label pop album, beaten to the punch by Ry Cooder's July 1979 album *Bop till You Drop*, which included the Chaka Khan duet "Don't Mess Up a Good Thing."

The result of this innovation is a decidedly disappointing album. At the time of release, it was both lauded and criticized for its experimentation and generally cringed at for its lyrical sentiments. While there has been some critical reappraisal of the work, which always happens, and defense of the album by Wonder apologists, which also always happens, it just doesn't work listening to it decades later.

Simply as recorded audio, it's awkward. As with Stevie's earlier "innervisions" or "music of his mind," we're invited into portraits of his internal thought process. But where the classic album portraits feel like a visit to the Louvre in which you were allowed to touch everything, even the *Mona Lisa*, this feels like a school-trip visit to the local art gallery where you're mostly just happy to not be in school, but not really happy about being made to view art. Alternately, most of the album feels like watching a Hollywood movie from the first days of synchronized sound, having to endure a hackneyed plotline made worse by a stationary camera, stunted dialogue, and wondering if the microphone is hidden in the flowers on the table between two actors.

Eight of the twenty tracks are instrumentals, and one of the remaining tracks, "Come Back as a Flower," features Syreeta on lead vocals. Earlier versions of the album had more instrumentals, and we all probably would have been better off if that had been maintained. Steve Loder says guitarist Michael Sembello's lyrics on "Flower Power" "score a cringe factor of 119 percent," and the words Wonder offers "range from the naïve to the unintelligible to, to the incomprehensible and beyond the unfathomably mawkish." Ouch.

The lyrics were added and tracks moved around after distributors Paramount Pictures balked at offering the film a wide release after a one-week Academy screening in December 1978 at Los Angeles' Mann Bruin Theater: Stevie had to add more songs for Mr. Gordy to release this on its own. The film everyone saw? Some interesting footage of Stevie walking around in nature, and as one blogger has put it, "the film is sprinkled with cool visuals to watch while baked!" To that end, many showings of the film have occurred on April 20.

Wonder released three singles from the album. "Send One Your Love" is a harmless if uninspiring single that, not surprisingly, topped the US adult contemporary (read: easy listening or dentist waiting room) charts. Stevie's harmonica on this song seems lazy, recalling all the lounge-friendly bursts from many tepid mid-1960s sides. "Black Orchid" was released in Europe and the UK, where it was backed by the sardonic inclusion of "Blame It on the Sun" as a B-side. "Outside My Window" sputtered in the mid-1950s on the US pop and R&B charts. It's got charming touches of 1960s Motown, but the chippy instrumentation is annoying.

The album reached number four on both the pop and R&B charts, riding on the coattails of Stevie's reputation more than the quality of the music. Famously, this is one of those late 1970s/early 1980s albums that purportedly shipped gold and returned platinum. Record labels and distributors would give serious discounts on bulk shipments to record stores, not only to get money up front but also to get publicity and, before the system was changed, important sales certifications. But the *Secret Life of Plants* and other albums, most notably the four simultaneously released Kiss solo albums in 1979, 1978's *Sgt. Pepper's Lonely Hearts Club Band*, which featured the Bee Gees and Peter Frampton, and Fleetwood Mac's *Tusk* (1979), all grossly undersold industry and shipping estimates. All of these discs populated record stores' cut-price cutout bins (albums with a slice through the cover indicating that they shouldn't be sold at full price—a visual marker of the label's tax write-off) for years to come. The bargain it afforded, and not the music or the monochromatic cover, was what first attracted me to the LP.

THE WOMAN IN RED

Stevie's next foray into soundtracks was 1984's *The Woman in Red*. If you have any doubt that Wonder was involved with the music for this weaker remake of the 1977 French comedy *Pardon Mon Affaire*, his name appears seven times on the front cover. Thanks, Mr. Gordy.

Stevie was brought onto the project by longtime friend Dionne Warwick, who shared vocals with Stevie on two songs and with whom he would soon record "That's What Friends Are For." Like producer Braun on the previous soundtrack, Warwick watched the movie with Stevie and described what she saw. He went home and created songs to match the mood.

The result wasn't quite the full-blown Stevie LP follow-up to 1980's *Hotter Than July* that some were waiting for—that would have to wait for 1985's *In Square Circle*, which Stevie was sitting on. But it was a commercially successful collection of adequate Stevie songs that would set the stage for the rest of Stevie's recording career. It's got the consistent post-mid-1980s fault of relying too much on gimmicky synthesizers at the expense of more complex, organic songwriting, mixed with sentimental and painfully naïve lyrics. Still, as with the bulk of the last forty years of his career, it's not something you can simply dismiss, but neither is it a go-to selection in Wonder's canon.

The first single from the LP, "I Just Called to Say I Love You" has warranted its own chapter in this book. The second single, "Love Light in Flight" gets some serious appreciation by Wonder fans, and the slight funk can be catchy, but there's no modulation in the sound—it never really goes anywhere. It hit number four on the R&B charts.

The third single, "Don't Drive Drunk," is an odd track. Musically, it's a synthetically busy song that fits in more with California new wave—think Danny Elfman and his band Oingo Boingo—than with contemporaneous R&B. It's got some aural life to it. Lyrically, it's a wash. In sentiment, it's a laudable anti-drinking-and-driving song; in execution, it's tragically unhip, and the callout to Mothers Against Drunk Driving is cheap. Its simplicity almost makes "Ebony and Ivory" seem like a well-theorized investigation of race relations.

Stevie had first dipped his toes in the 12-inch/remix stream with two worthwhile versions of "Master Blaster (Jammin')" in 1980. He continued that with "Love Light in Flight" and "Don't Drive Drunk," which featured a remix of *Hotter Than July*'s "Did I Hear You Say You Love Me" on the 12-inch B-side, and through his last major single, 2005's "So What the Fuss."

JUNGLE FEVER

Stevie released his third and final soundtrack in 1991 with songs to accompany Spike Lee's fifth major studio film, *Jungle Fever*. The movie is the story of a married Black architect (Wesley Snipes) who becomes involved with a white woman (Annabella Sciorra). Hilarity doesn't ensue as much as prejudices and assumptions about interracial dating are explored, more like the "Black issues" Stevie eventually thought he'd investigate in soundtrack work rather than plant telekinesis.

Spike Lee and Stevie had worked together in the past. Stevie wrote "I Can Only Be Me" for Spike's second studio film, *School Daze*. It was performed for the film by Keith John, who has appeared as a background singer on all of Stevie's releases after 1985.

According to a 2016 *Slate* interview, Lee went into the movie knowing he wanted to use "Living for the City." While it's not on the soundtrack LP, he considers it part of the soundtrack. The song appears in one of the most pivotal scenes, when Snipes searches the netherworld for his junkie brother, played by Samuel L. Jackson. When it came time to create a soundtrack, he told Stevie, "I want your next album to be *Jungle Fever*." Unlike the visual prompts for *The Secret Life of Plants*, Wonder this time used a Braille script to read the movie, augmented by an assistant providing visual details. In the end, Lee thinks that "Stevie hit it out of the park."

Jungle Fever was Stevie's third LP release in the seven years since *The Woman in Red*. *In Square Circle* followed quickly in 1985. Like its predecessor, and *Characters*, which would follow two years later, it doesn't have much to recommend for or against it. If this were the first time you heard this performer, you might be intrigued, but not enough to return to the music. Because it's Stevie, it's worth a second listen. But often it sounds vaguely like songs in the background of a John Hughes teen comedy: mid-eighties midlife crisis music.

In Square Circle, which hit pop number five and R&B number one, offered four US singles, all of which would reach the R&B top 20, with the innocuous "Part-Time Lover," a watered-down copy of "You Can't Hurry Love," hitting number one the pop and R&B charts. "Go Home" reached number two R&B, while the ballad "Overjoyed," the best song on the album despite some annoying production quirks, hit number eight. Final single "Land of La La" sounds like the kind of music performers on *Dancing with the Stars* would use.

Characters (1987) was more of the same, if slightly funkier, hitting number one on the R&B chart. It was the first of Wonder's LPs to fail to reach the US pop top five since *Music of My Mind*. The album featured six singles stretched out over two years, including the Europe-only "Free." The lead single "Skeletons" took on Ronald Reagan, Oliver Stone, and Iran Contra, much like mid-seventies singles confronted Richard Nixon, and was rewarded with a number-one R&B hit. The somnambulistic ballad "You Will Know" followed it to number one. The Michael Jackson duet "Get It" hit number four, and "My Eyes Don't Cry" hit number six.

Echoing *In Square Circle*'s "It's Wrong (Apartheid)," Stevie released the non-LP anti-apartheid ballad "Keep Our Love Alive," which hit number 24 on the R&B chart. While he didn't quite hit the high notes, the July 30, 2009, version at Mandela Day 2009 from Radio City Music Hall is a much more moving version.

Jungle Fever, released May 28, 1991, is the most completely conceived and most enjoyable of Stevie's post-1980 work (although some favor *Conversation Peace*). As with the New Power Generation and Prince album of the same year, *Diamonds and Pearls*, it enters a world in which hip-hop exists among the many R&B stylistic choices, even if neither album quite gets them all right.

And, thankfully, it doesn't all sound like mannered variations on the same recycled synthesizer riff. Some of that might be credited to the reappearance of Malcolm Cecil, who's credited with additional engineering and additional programming. Little Stevie needed an adult in the recording room and you can't help but wonder if the 1980s and 1990s would have been more successful with another voice in the studio to push back at Stevie.

And the album is fun! In fact, the opening track is literally called "Fun Day." "Fun Day" is the album's standout track. It's one of the few jazz-oriented tunes among Stevie's latter work, and it beats anything on *Eivets Rednow*. It's got a plush vocal, features a sweet harmonica solo, and, surprisingly, a brief piano solo. Ribowsky adds that the track has an "aural lingua of deep-seated funk" through "hip-hop 'African' percussion," which I think means it's R&B that doesn't sound the same as all the other stuff he was creating at the same time.

For all this, the released version of "Fun Day" still suffers from some of the worst tendencies of late-1980s/early-1990s production—it doesn't really feel human. A much superior version was broadcast in 1991 on ABC's short-lived late-night show *Into the*

Night with Rick Dees. It's got Stevie on piano backed by a real band with live drums and background singers. The joyful nature of the song shines through, and for all the clichés and eventual inevitability of "unplugged" sessions at this time, you wish Stevie had given us an LP of songs with just him and the piano or a session with a live acoustic band.

In addition to chatting with "Disco Duck" creator Dees, Stevie and his band also performed a medley of the title track and the first single, "Gotta Have You." As with "Fun Day," both better the already enjoyable LP versions, with "Gotta Have You" thankfully avoiding the up-front synth bass and drums. "Gotta Have You" hit number three on the R&B charts, Wonder's last top-five R&B single; it hit number 92 on the pop charts, one of three top-100 pop hits post 1987 (1995's "For Your Love" and 2005's "So What the Fuss" the others). "Fun Day" hit number six on the R&B chart, and the third single, the ballad "These Three Words," was his last top-10 R&B single.

"Chemical Love" is also a fan favorite from the album. It's almost experimental with its tampered synths and mostly monotone vocals, but it also recalls Steve Winwood's "Higher Love" at times.

While these three albums are the only soundtracks that carry the Stevie Wonder name, Stevie has participated in a few additional soundtrack endeavors.

The most enjoyable soundtrack song is "Upset Stomach" from Motown's film production *The Last Dragon*. In a case of the expert following the pupil, Stevie creates an angular, six-plus-minute synth-dance track that sounds like a decent outtake from Prince's *1999*.

In 1996 he contributed two original songs to the soundtrack of Steve Barron's *The Adventures of Pinocchio*, the director's take on the classic (and terrifying) story of a puppet that's brought to life. Barron was a regular in music circles in the 1980s, have conceived and directed three iconic videos: Michael Jackson's "Billie Jean," Dire Straits' animated "Money for Nothing," and A-ha's quasi-animated "Take on Me." Unfortunately, both ballads are forgettable and stretched beyond usefulness on the LP and in the movie, in which they're a bit incongruous with the tenor of Italy in the 1700s. The single "Kiss Lonely Good-Bye" also features on the albums in orchestra and harmonica-and-orchestra versions, and "Hold Onto Your Dream" also features in an orchestra version. They got their money's worth out of Stevie.

At this point, Stevie's soundtrack contributions are more guest appearances than true creative projects. He joined 98 Degrees on "True to Your Heart," the theme song and first single from Disney's 1998 animated *Mulan*. This single, as with the Pinocchio songs, seemed at odds with the overall film and failed to chart. 98 Degrees would hit the top of the US pop charts two years later with "Thank God I Found You," along with Mariah Carey and Joe. Joe would feature on Stevie's 2023 single "Don't Make Me Wait Too Long," which also featured Kimberly Brewer, who sang lead vocals on *Jungle Fever*'s "If She Breaks Your Heart."

Chapter Nine Playlist

"Don't Mess Up a Good Thing," Ry Cooder

"Flower Power," Stevie Wonder

"Don't Drive Drunk," Stevie Wonder

"I Can Only Be Me," Keith John

"Overjoyed," Stevie Wonder

"Skeletons," Stevie Wonder

"Keep Our Love Alive," Stevie Wonder

"Gotta Have You," Stevie Wonder

"Chemical Love," Stevie Wonder

"Upset Stomach," Stevie Wonder

"Kiss Lonely Good-Bye" (orchestra), Stevie Wonder

10

"SO WHAT THE FUSS"

Collaborations

By design, working at Motown in the 1960s was an all-hands on-deck collaborative experience. Stevie not only sang and performed on his own records, but he also played on other artists', and he eventually cowrote and coproduced songs before heading in the other direction and doing everything by himself in the early 1970s. The pendulum swung back, and eventually, Stevie was again collaborating with other artists more often than he wasn't.

This chapter looks at some of his major work with other artists, focusing on 2005's "So What the Fuss," a collaboration with Prince and En Vogue and his last chart single.

THE BACKSTORY

Jungle Fever was followed by *Conversation Peace* in 1995. *Conversation Peace* evolved from an extended 1993 stay in Ghana. It "is an album dedicated to finding peace in a world full of mistrust, hate,

and violence," according to Perrone. While this worldview conflat-
ing universal and personal struggles doesn't sharply distinguish it
from earlier work, its social justice propensities won the approval of
critics. Megadeth be damned, peace does sell.

More suspect was Wonder's further integration of hip-hop and
other contemporary sounds. It's a catch-22 for a mature artist: stick
to your sound and you're a dinosaur, update your sound and you're
following trends. Ultimately, *Conversation Peace* is an LP that critics
want to like because it's Stevie, but there's rationalization necessary
to get to the point of liking it.

The American public liked Stevie well enough to boost the LP
to number 16 on the pop charts and number two R&B. The album
rendered four singles, three of which were released in the United
States. The MOR lead single "For Your Love" hit number 11 R&B,
his last top 20 on that chart; it hit number 53 on the pop chart,
his highest entry since "Skeletons" in 1987. Stevie's dancehall entry
"Tomorrow Robins Will Sing" and R&B/boy band–influenced
"Treat Myself" both snuck into the top 100. "Cold Chill," one of a
handful of Stevie songs that vaguely sounds like a cousin of Bobby
Brown's "My Prerogative," was only released in Europe.

Live dates in the United States, Japan, the Middle East, and
Europe ensued, with the November 1995 double LP *Natural Wonder* culled from Osaka and Tel Aviv dates.

Natural Wonder was followed by a decade gap until *A Time to
Love*, released September 27, 2005. It's a stronger album than *Conversation Peace*, more diverse musically, and it simply fits in with

the contemporary music scene by not trying so hard to fit in. The highlights include the power ballad "Shelter in the Rain," a tribute to Syreeta, who had died of cancer the previous year, the light jazz of "Moon Blue," and the lead single "So What the Fuss."

The album equaled the previous studio album on the R&B chart, hitting number two, but bettered *Conversation Peace* at number five pop. The album had four singles. "From the Bottom of My Heart," a thin "I Just Called to Say I Love You" rewrite, hit number 52 R&B and won Stevie a 2006 Grammy Award for Best Male Pop Vocal Performance.

"Shelter in the Rain" single proceeds went to the Wonder Foundation for Hurricane Katrina, the 2005 US Gulf Coast hurricane that killed over eighteen hundred people. The upbeat, reggae-tinged "Positivity," featuring daughter Aisha Morris, subject of 1976's "Isn't She Lovely," was released in Europe.

As of this writing, *A Time to Love* is Wonder's last album of new material. Its distribution was followed two weeks later by the release of *The Complete Stevie Wonder*, a nearly forty-hour compilation of Stevie's "solo" work for Motown. But it's his work with others that we're tackling here.

THE SONG

"So What the Fuss" was the lead single from *A Time to Love*. It's Stevie's last single to chart on both the pop and R&B charts, hitting 96 on the former and a modest 34 on the latter. It's a slinky, funky-but-bright soul song featuring En Vogue on background vocals and Prince on guitar.

Lyrically, Stevie catalogs a hecka-lotta things that can go wrong, from forgetting to wear shoes to failing to vote, to showing up at a restaurant in Klantown. He then assigns blame to me, us, and them for each infraction. Stevie gets about as naughty as he did on "Ain't Gonna Stand for It" ("somebody's been rubbing on my good luck charm," etc.), although there it was tongue in cheek, here it's tongue in check, throwing his arms up and editing himself: "so what the fuss?"

Nine different versions of the song were released, counting edits and remixes, including a version featuring a rap by Q-Tip of A Tribe Called Quest. Three of these remixes ended up on *The Complete Stevie Wonder* including the "Global Soul Remix."

Stevie played the song live for a few years. More memorable performances include the July 2, 2005, Live 8 performance from Philadelphia (designed to fight global poverty), the intimate November 9 show at Abbey Road Studios, and as part of a medley with "A Time to Love" on February 5, 2006, at Super Bowl XL.

The song is notable as the first music video with descriptive audio for blind viewers. The visual descriptions, akin to how Stevie watches movies, was provided by Busta Rhymes. Wonder would return the favor on Rhymes's 2006 LP *The Big Bang*, providing vocals on "Been through the Storm." Rhymes would also appear on Stevie's 2020 Black Lives Matter single "Can't Put It in the Hands of Fate." It was his first release after he left Motown, setting up shop with his own So What the Fuss Music label.

"So What the Fuss" is the only time Stevie Wonder and Prince appeared together on a released song, although Prince probably added instruments to the "Cold Chill (Prince Remix)," which found wide release in 2005 on *The Complete Stevie Wonder*.

Their most successful recorded collaboration was one they didn't work on together. Chaka Khan's 1984 R&B number-one Hot Black Single was a cover of Prince's 1979 album track "I Feel for You." The song features one of Wonder's signature chromatic harmonica solos and a vocal sample from "Fingertips—Part 2." It also includes rapping from Melle Mel of Grandmaster Flash and the Furious Five. The seminal rappers leaned heavily into Stevie on their 1982 debut LP *The Message*. The group covered Wonder's 1970 Spinners hit as "It's a Shame (Mt. Airy Groove)," and the mellow "Dreamin'" was a fanboy mash to Stevie: "We'd like to send this one all the way out to Stevie Wonder."

Wonder, Khan, and Prince played the song live together on June 27, 2006, at the BET Awards. The six-song set, celebrating Khan's Lifetime Achievement Award, included Prince on guitar and Stevie on keyboards. Unlike a lot of awards-show superstar mash-ups, it works.

As Black singers, songwriters, producers, and one-man bands, Stevie and Prince share headspace in the public imagination. Prince's original handler, Chris Moon, brought him to New York City to meet with record labels in fall 1976. Moon told labels he represented Stevie Wonder but was forced to admit that he represented the "new" Stevie Wonder. The following spring, Prince's first manager, Owen Husney, brought Prince to Los Angeles, again as the "new" Stevie Wonder, a "Black crossover artist who could write, produce, and play everything." Prince signed with Warner Bros. that spring.

Prince played about a dozen Stevie songs live, most often "Superstition." Most notably the two performed together at the Barack Obama White House on June 13, 2015, to celebrate African American Music Appreciation Month, playing, at least, Prince's "Kiss" and "Purple Rain" and Stevie's "Signed, Sealed, Delivered I'm Yours." The next evening Wonder joined Prince and his band 3rdeyegirl on five songs at Washington's Warner Theatre.

Prince showed up at multiple Stevie live shows over the years, most famously at a Paris Le Bercy show on July 1, 2010. And Stevie played a few Prince songs live, including the ballad "The Most Beautiful Girl in the World" at a handful of shows in 2007, "Take Me with U" in 2016 at the BET Awards, and an abbreviated "Purple Rain" with Madonna at the Billboard Music Awards on May 22, 2016, a month after Prince's death.

Just as Prince did in the 1980s, Stevie spent a lot of time during his early career collaborating. Throughout the 1960s Stevie played instruments on other Motown tracks, such as drums on the Four Tops' "Loving You Is Sweeter than Ever" (1966), and frequently cowrote with house writers before landing his first outside writing gig, "This Town," on Rotary Connection's 1969 LP *Songs*. Rotary Connection included singer Minnie Riperton.

Stevie's first outside production gig was for the Spinners' "It's a Shame" from their 1970 LP *2nd Time Around*. He also played on the song and cowrote it with Lee Garrett and Syreeta Wright. The smooth earworm hit number four on the Hot Soul chart.

Wonder's full-time plunge into outside production was on ex-wife Syreeta Wright's 1972 debut LP *Syreeta*. Stevie wrote or cowrote seven of the ten songs, including "I Love Every Little Thing about You," which appeared at the same time on *Music of My Mind*, and played most everything except guitar, bass, and drums. In other words, this is a Stevie album, save the vocals.

The LP's first single, "To Know You Is to Love You," is an epic, pre-disco pas de deux between Stevie, who gets the first verse, and Syreeta. It stacks up with the best of the Motown duets, but with a darker undercurrent that brings more weight to the proceedings. The three-minute single is amazing, the six-minute unfaded album version is among Stevie's best work.

Released June 19, 1974, *Stevie Wonder Presents: Syreeta* is a notch down from his debut production job, but not by much. Coming just a few weeks before the release of *Fulfillingness' First Finale*, it's an alternative vision of that LP. *Fulfillingness' Prelude? Prefillingness' First Finale?* As a contrast to Syreeta's debut, there's a full band backing her, essentially the Wonderlove touring band.

Stevie wrote or cowrote all eleven of the songs. The album's notable for the first appearance of "Cause We've Ended as Lovers," which Stevie subsequently gave to Jeff Beck, and the fourth single "Your Kiss Is Sweet," which an eleven-year-old Björk covered in her native Icelandic as "Búkolla." "Búkolla" is a mythical speaking cow. It's an extraordinarily long three-and-a-half-minute listen.

Wonder's last complete outside production album was Minnie Riperton's *Perfect Angel* release in August 1974, two months after the Syreeta and Wonder LPs. Stevie, as El Toro Negro, coproduced the LP with Riperton's husband Richard Rudolph, forming the one-off Scorbu Productions. Stevie wrote two songs, "Take a Little Trip" (on which he's way up in the vocal mix) and the title song. The album was Riperton's bestseller, and it includes the number-one pop hit "Lovin' You," her high-range vocals sitting over Stevie's swirling synths on a lullaby to the couple's young daughter, actor Maya Rudolph (who's currently in the best all-female Prince cover band, Princess).

OTHER COLLABORATIONS

A Time to Love also included contributions from India.Arie and Paul McCartney on the title track. Stevie and India.Arie previously worked together on bonus tracks for her 2002 LP *Voyage to India*, named after the plush sitar-via-synthesizer instrumental track on *Stevie Wonder's Journey through "The Secret Life of Plants."* Wonder contributed vocals to the "Christmas Song (Chestnuts Roasting on an Open Fire)," which he originally recorded for 1967's *Someday at Christmas*. He coproduced the track with Terry Lewis, coproducer with Jimmy Jam on a gazillion hits for Janet Jackson; both Jam and Lewis were members of the Prince-manipulated group the Time.

In addition to the 1982 collaborations "Ebony and Ivory" and "What's That You're Doing?" from McCartney's *Tug of War*, Stevie contributed harmonica to "Only Our Hearts" on Paul's 2012 LP *Kisses on the Bottom*. Wonder and McCartney first met in London in 1966. The next year Wonder would meet fellow American Jimi Hendrix and jam with the Jimi Hendrix Experience on two songs for the BBC's *Top Gear* radio program, the Hendrix original "Jammin'" and "I Was Made to Love Her." Stevie's on drums. He and Jimi sound like they're having a duel and a whole bunch of fun. The songs are on the 1998 Hendrix collection *BBC Sessions*.

While his early 1970s bands can rock and Wonderlove was nothing less than competent, these recordings make me wish Stevie had spent more time working with other rock/funk musicians—challenging himself rather than being supported. There's a clip online of a short drum bit backed by Italian prog-rock band Formula 3 that makes you want even more of this type of musical interaction.

Alas, most of Stevie's collaborations are not barn-burning prog-rock experiments but more along the lines of material such as "Ebony and Ivory," including duets with Frank Sinatra and Gladys Knight, Barbra Streisand, and Bono. This is not surprising since his prime collaboration period was the mid-1980s, aka the era of "I Just Called to Say I Love You." While this period included the upbeat "I Feel for You," it tended more toward ballads.

"Stay Gold" is cowritten with Oscar winner Carmine Coppola for his son Francis Ford Coppola's 1983 adaptation of *The Outsiders*. It's a plaintive ballad that's an engaging song on its own, but one that's incongruous with the rest of the film and tucked away over the end credits. The alternative version, cleaner and with Stevie in better vocal form, is superior. It can be found on the 2013 thirtieth-anniversary album release.

Stevie added one of his most iconic harmonica solos to Elton John's 1983 "I Guess That's Why They Call It the Blues" from *Too Low for Zero*. In 1993 Stevie on harmonica joined Sir Elton on the Wonder original "Go On and On" for John's *Duets*. Producer Stevie Wonder did no one any favors on this creaky track.

The year 1985 was huge for Stevie and group collaboration/charity work. In January he took part in the USA for Africa collaboration to raise money for Ethiopian famine relief. Stevie was brought in by organizers Kenny Rogers and Lionel Richie for curb appeal. He thought he'd help write the song, "We Are the World," but Richie and Michael Jackson had already done so by the time he showed up.

Wonder was central to the January 28, 1985, final vocal recording at A&M Recording Studios in Hollywood. He acted as unofficial greeter and class cutup, threatening artists that if they didn't complete their lines in one take, he and Ray Charles would drive them home. He caused some controversy by trying to introduce some Swahili to the lyrics, offending good ol' boy Waylon Jennings and causing others to question if Ethiopians even spoke Swahili (they don't).

A writer for *The Guardian*, reviewing the 2024 documentary *The Greatest Night in Pop* about the making of the song, said of the controversy, "An ensuing debate over whether the people of Ethiopia, which was particularly affected by famine, speak Amharic or Swahili will resonate with anybody who has found themselves in a dysfunctional group Zoom." There is no Swahili in the final version, but Jennings sings in the large chorus.

Bob Dylan gets a few lines to himself, but he had trouble getting there. Reversing the usual role when Stevie needs a Vocal Whisperer to provide lyrics, Wonder helped the "Blowin' in the Wind" writer manage his part. Maybe Bob was too tired from recording "Seeing the Real You at Last," one of his best mid-1980s songs, earlier in the day.

Wonder gets two lines in the opening stanza, and the song rides on the chart-topping backs of post–"I Just Called to Say I Love You" Stevie and post–*Born in the U.S.A.* Bruce Springsteen trading lines in the chorus ("We are the world / We are the children").

The single was released March 7, 1985. It raised over $80 million (over $200 million in 2020s money), provided some relief to Ethiopians, and ushered in a controversial neoliberal era of Western musical artists raising money for all manner of "good causes." It went to number one in multiple global markets, although it stalled at number 72 on the country charts in the United States, perhaps due to Waylon Jennings's bad vibes.

The single was followed by the Live Aid concert on July 13, 1985, a joint famine relief effort held simultaneously in London and Philadelphia. Stevie turned down an offer to participate because he didn't want to be the token Black guy. From where I was standing in Philadelphia, no one cared about Patti LaBelle or Ashford & Simpson, but Run-D.M.C. were actively booed.

Later in 1985, Wonder joined Dionne Warwick, Elton John, and Gladys Knight for Dionne and Friends' recording of "That's What Friends Are For." Stevie sings and plays harmonica on the single that hit number one on the pop and R&B charts and raised over $3 million for the American Foundation for AIDS Research. The quartet won the Grammy Award for Best Pop Performance by a Duo or Group with Vocals, and songwriters Burt Bacharach (well known to Warwick and Wonder) and Carole Bayer Sager won Song of the Year.

Among less lofty collaborations, Stevie was writer, producer, vocalist, and instrumentalist on Whitney Houston's "We Didn't Know." It's a soft tune that was the sixth and final single from Houston's 1990 four-times-platinum *I'm Your Baby Tonight*.

Many of the younger persuasion know Wonder best from his 2016 collaboration with Ariana Grande, "Faith," from *Sing: Original Motion Picture Soundtrack*. The film and deluxe version of soundtrack also include a cover of "Don't You Worry 'bout a Thing," which helped cement the song's popularity as a glee club/a cappella standard.

Since 2016 and "Faith," Stevie has released four non-LP singles, all featuring other artists, and has appeared on six songs by other artists. At this point it's hard to see him going out on his own again. But that's what friends are for.

Chapter Ten Playlist

"Been through the Storm," Busta Rhymes

"I Feel for You," Chaka Khan

"Dreamin'," Grandmaster Flash and the Furious Five

"Loving You Is Sweeter than Ever," The Four Tops

"This Town," Rotary Connection

"It's a Shame," The Spinners

"To Know You Is to Love You" (unedited), Syreeta

"Búkolla," Björk

"Take a Little Trip," Minnie Riperton

"We Didn't Know," Whitney Houston

"Faith," Stevie Wonder featuring Ariana Grande

11

"SIR DUKE"

Live Shows

The Complete Stevie Wonder release in 2005 effectively marked the beginning of Stevie's semi-retirement from the recording industry. Yes, he still released some music and played some live dates, but clearly, he was more a fifty-five-year-old picking up some hours greeting people at Walmart than a nine-to-five investment banker putting in eighty-hour weeks. And a lot of what he's done in the past two decades has been greeting people, often celebrities, but also regular people. And as his musical production has ebbed, this giving has flowed, as he's actively worked with dozens of charities, including the Barbara Davis Center for Childhood Diabetes, Habitat for Humanity, the Special Olympics, and the United Negro College Fund. For all this, he's received countless accolades, including being named a United Nations Messenger of Peace in 2009 and a French Commander of Arts and Letters in 2010, and receiving the US Presidential Medal of Freedom in 2014. He is an honorable and honored man.

But he did work during this time. While there were no new LPs and only a smattering of individual tracks on his own and with others, he did stay on the road. While many of his live performances were one-offs for charity and awards shows, he embarked on a number of global jaunts and greatest hits jams, such as 2007–2008's A Wonder Summer's Night and 2018–2019's The Stevie Wonder Song Party.

But the most important tour post-2005 tour was the 2014–2015 *Songs in the Key of Life* performance tour. The tour stretched out over forty-plus dates from a November 6, 2014, Madison Square Garden stop to a November 24, 2015, MSG return gig, topped by a British Summer Time 2016 show in London's Hyde Park on July 10, 2016.

These shows are important because Stevie never gave *Songs in the Key of Life* its due after it was first released in November 1976. The subsequent two years saw Stevie performing at a handful of one-off dates. By 1979 he was on to a *Secret Life of Plants* mini tour, followed in 1980 by a more expansive *Hotter Than July* excursion.

This concluding chapter takes a look at Stevie's released live work, pivoting on "Sir Duke" and the *Songs in the Key of Life* victory lap.

THE BACKSTORY

Stevie Wonder has released four live albums.

Even on record, Stevie first made his name with his commanding live performances. Stevie's first live album, *Recorded Live: The*

12 Year Old Genius (1963), was also his first major success. The LP, and its number-one single, "Fingertips—Part 2," is covered thoroughly in the first chapter, so no need to linger here.

Since then he's released three more live albums plus a smattering of 1960s Motown-package live recordings. For a sixty-plus-year career, this is a crime, especially considering that two of the albums came out at the same time in 1970.

Stevie Wonder Live was released in the United States on March 6, 1970. It received an international release at this time, including in the Netherlands, where it was titled *Live in Person on Tour in USA*, and Argentina, where it was renamed *Ayer Yo, Ayer Tu, Ayer = Live* to capitalize on the recent single "Yester-Me, Yester-You, Yesterday." The Dutch "USA" moniker was accurate as the album was recorded live at the Roostertail in Detroit on December 19, 1969.

The Roostertail is a Detroit landmark that sits on the Detroit River across from Belle Isle. In 1966 it started hosting Motown Mondays, live performances broadcast on the radio. The first performers were the Four Tops, with their 1966 LP *Four Tops Live* pulled from the show. *Temptations Live!* followed in 1967, as well as parts of Rare Earth and George Carlin live LPs.

The album's fifteen tracks are a disappointing mix of hits ("My Cherie Amour," "A Place in the Sun"), low-wattage LP tracks ("Sunny," "Down to Earth"), contemporary cover songs, and a precious few places where Stevie breaks loose. The pumped-up applause and Vegas orchestration can be tough to take. It's like watching a sitcom with a laugh track after you've experienced a single-camera show like *Seinfeld*.

Stevie would continue to perform fun cover songs throughout his career, but the three here are too-safe choices. They groove a bit, but not enough to offend or trouble the audience. "Love Theme from Romeo & Juliet (A Time for Us)" is a beautiful tune, yes, but, like the later "Alfie," it's little more than easy listening.

Originally released in 1967 by writer Fred Neil, future Wonderpal Harry Nilsson had a 1968 top-ten hit with the well-crafted "Everybody's Talkin'," but the adventuresomeness of the choice is at best questionable as Stevie's version was at least the thirtieth in less than two years.

Glen Campbell had the 1967 hit single with the Jimmy Webb classic "By the Time I Get to Phoenix," but the song was most memorably and disruptively delivered by Isaac Hayes in his eighteen-minute, forty-second rendition from 1969. Stevie interpreting standards or unimaginative choices? All three of these songs have each been covered over three hundred times.

So where does Stevie break loose? He cooks on the clavinet on "Shoo-Re-Doo-Be-Doo-Da-Day" and takes the gloves off on the drums on a cover of "Ca' Purange." He would continue to play drum solos in some form throughout his career.

"Ca' Purange" first appeared on tenor saxophonist Gene Ammons's 1962 Prestige LP *Bad! Bossa Nova* and was released as a single the same year. On the album liner notes Ammons (presumably) recounts a group trip to the Amazon, with the phrase "ca' purange" part of a chant that accompanied a drum groove from a Colombian Indigenous group. It's unclear what the phrase means, but it's been metaphorically translated to mean "jungle soul." The song was most famously covered by fellow tenor saxophonist Dexter Gordon on his 1973 LP *Ca' Purange*. The version found on that disc is otherworldly.

"Ca' Purange" was written by Mussapere, a pseudonym for Brazilian Natalicio Lima. Lima, along with his brother, Antenor, also known as Herundy, formed the northeast Brazilian duo Los Indios Tabajaras. This has been roughly translated as both Lords of the Indian Village and Indians from Northeastern Brazil.

The group has a performance and recording history stretching back to the early 1950s but was "discovered" by guitar wizard Chet Atkins and signed to RCA in 1958, releasing *Sweet and Savage*. The first Brazilians on the US pop charts, the group was on the charts for fourteen weeks and had a number-six pop hit in November 1963 with "Maria Elena." The song is a gentle classical piece in which, on first listen, the guitar could be mistaken for a zither.

Stevie Wonder Live reached number 16 on the R&B charts and only 83 on the pop charts. Frustratingly, there is no band credited, although the MC is Detroit DJ Scott Regen.

Stevie would release a UK-only live LP, *"Live" at the Talk of the Town* in October 1970. It's culled from a multiweek summer residence at the former London Hippodrome, which currently houses a casino and theater.

The LP duplicates five songs from the previous live album, including "Ca' Purange" credited here as "Drum Solo" with Wonder receiving writing credit. Overall, it's as uninspiring as the American disc, more a curio than a triumph. It does feature the two 1970 singles, the old-time Motown lilt of "Never Had a Dream Come True," and the rollicking album closer "Signed, Sealed, Delivered I'm Yours." The requisite safe, AM cover song is Simon & Garfunkel's "Bridge over Troubled Water" . . . which has been recorded almost seven hundred times.

Between *Recorded Live* in 1963 and the pair of 1970 albums, Stevie released (or, more accurately, had released) over a dozen live tracks pulled from Motown package shows.

The Motor-Town Revue Vol. 1—Recorded Live at the Apollo (1963) is a ten-track album pulled from December 1962 dates on the second Motor-Town Revue. The recording happened a few weeks after James Brown recorded his October 24 Apollo show that would render his first *Live at the Apollo* (1963) album, considered by many as the greatest live LP of all time. Brown would follow with four more Apollo albums over the years. Other artists who released Apollo albums include B. B. King and Hall and Oates, featuring ex-Temptations David Ruffin and Eddie Kendricks.

Little Stevie Wonder's Apollo contribution is a looser version of Ray Charles's "Don't You Know" than the *Recorded Live* offering and much better than the *Tribute to Uncle Ray* version.

The following year saw the release of *Recorded Live the Motortown Revue Vol. 2* (1964) This was recorded November 17, 1963, at the Fox Theatre in Detroit. Stevie dips back to his first single, "I Call It Pretty Music, but the Old People Call It the Blues," for some R&B flavor and then hits the Mancini/Mercer classic from *Breakfast at Tiffany's*, "Moon River," which has been recorded over a thousand times. I'm partial to Morrissey's version.

Stevie's third live compilation appearance was on 1965's *Motortown Revue in Paris*, recorded at the Olympia on April 13, 1965. This is the strongest of the four Motortown Revue collections, with the Supremes and the Miracles both in top-notch form. Stevie's contributions, "High Heel Sneakers" (which reached number 30 on the R&B chart), Willie Nelson's "Funny How Time Slips Away," and another "Fingertips," were covered in chapter 2. A 2016 European/Japanese Deluxe Edition added Stevie's opening number, the fun "Jazz-Blues Instrumental," and a by-the-books version of "Make Someone Happy" from *With a Song in My Heart*.

The final Motortown package was in 1969 with the defeatist title *Motortown Revue Live*, recorded late 1968 at Detroit's Fox Theatre. The LP features Gladys Knight & the Pips, and most of the old guard is gone, save the Temptations with their psychedelic anthem "Cloud Nine." For Stevie, no surprises here, just the recent hits "For Once in My Life" and "Shoo-Re-Doo-Be-Doo-Da-Day," which would both appear on both 1970s live discs, and old favorite "Uptight (Everything's Alright)." And thus ends the Motortown Revue.

Wonder also appeared on two joint Motown live compilations. He shared the 1968 *Tamla-Motown Festival Tokyo '68* Japan-only album with Martha Reeves and the Vandellas. It was recorded at the Shibuya Public Hall in Tokyo, Japan, on February 13, 1968.

The venue, now named Line Cube Shibuya, has been a favorite venue for both legal and bootleg recordings, with releases from the Temptations, Weather Report, and the Runaways.

Stevie opens with a frenetic version of Leslie Bricusse and Anthony Newley's "Feeling Good" from their 1964 production *The Roar of the Greasepaint—The Smell of the Crowd*. Nina Simone released a notable, much slower version in 1965, and it would serve as George Michael's last single while he was alive, in 2014. John Legend performed the song as a vampy spiritual in front of the Lincoln Memorial on January 20, 2021, at the Biden/Harris Presidential Inauguration.

"Feeling Good" would appear on the Japanese B-side for the live "A Place in the Sun." The other four LP tracks are A-sides that appear on other live releases above, although the recording here is superior to most of the American-recorded shows.

The final Motown live comp for Stevie was 1970's *Motown at the Hollywood Palace*. It captures the live October 18, 1969, broadcast of the weekly ABC TV show *The Hollywood Palace*. The show, which ran from 1964 to 1970, didn't have a fixed host. Diana Ross hosted the program that evening. Other hosts that season included Milton Berle, Don Knotts, and Burt Bacharach with Angie Dickinson (what?). The album includes material from Gladys Knight & the Pips and the Jackson 5, but leans heavily on Diana Ross and the Supremes in one of their homestretch live appearances together.

Stevie got a nine-minute slot on the broadcast. He and Ross duet on two numbers, "I'm Gonna Make You Love Me" and Stevie's then go-to live song "For Once in My Life." The former song was a 1968 number-two pop and R&B hit for the joint Diana Ross and the Supremes and the Temptations group, and each group featured it on subsequent live albums. Stevie takes the Eddie Kendricks part in a jocular interpretation of the tune and cooks on the harmonica.

Ruling from his clavinet, Stevie performed a striking version of the *For Once in My Life* single "I Don't Know Why," here titled "Don't Know Why I Love You." While there is an audience in some of the broadcast shots, beyond the vocals the "live" aspect of all this is questionable. But it's still great.

And even greater is a performance of the song on UK's *Top of the Pops*, broadcast March 3, 1969. It's got a much fuller orchestral backing, bringing forth the dark gravity of the song. Stevie starts at the clavinet but stands up with his microphone and wails. It sends shivers down my spine, even if the clean-cut audience members somehow rounded up in London in 1969 barely notice.

From 1970, jump forward to November 21, 1995, and the release of the double-LP *Natural Wonder*, to date the only live album that features Stevie as a mature artist. It picks up where the 1970s discs left off, with "My Cherie Amour" and "Signed, Sealed, Delivered I'm Yours," the only old-school Stevie singles included.

The thirteen-track first disc offers slightly less-known songs, such as "Rocket Love" and "Tomorrow Robins Will Sing," alongside three new tracks, the very long opener "Dancing to the Rhythm"; "Ms. & Mr. Little Ones," an outtake from *Conversation Peace*; and "Stevie Ray Blues," a tribute to Stevie Ray Vaughan, who died in a 1990 plane crash. Stevie Ray and B. B. King had featured on a *Characters* CD bonus track, "Come Let Me Make Your Love Come Down." Stevie also performs "Stay Gold" from *The Outsiders* and "Pastime Paradise," which had enjoyed a 1995 revival with Coolio's number-one pop sample/cover "Gangsta's Paradise," featuring L.V.

The second disc featured eleven hit singles that alone could constitute a greatest hits album—you can probably name at least half of them without looking.

The songs were recorded on March 1, 1995, at Osaka-jou Hall in Japan, backed by the Tokyo Philharmonic Orchestra, and in August 1995 in Tel Aviv, Israel. It was Stevie's first visit to the Holy Land, and he was feted with honors in Jerusalem and Tel Aviv as he toured the historic cities.

Somewhat predictably, the album itself comes off as sterile and somewhat perfunctory. The performances are well executed and safe, about what you'd expect from a performer at this stage of his career. A souvenir of past performances, but not something to remember in and of itself.

THE SONG

The "Sir Duke" performance on *Natural Wonder* is rushed, about a minute briefer than the studio version, and suffers from a thin, trebly mix that's compounded by the too-loud mastering of mid-1990s CDs. For all that, it's difficult to deny the energy, optimism, and hope that permeates the song and makes it not just a celebration of music—and more precisely a celebration of a subset of twentieth-century American jazz musicians—but a celebration of life.

In *A Musical Guide to the Classic Albums*, analyzing the studio version, Steve Loder explains the song's musical appeal as such: "primarily the groove, then the unexpected melodic and harmonic twist in the chorus, and the immaculate horn section arrangement." I'd also add in the vocal phrasing.

Of course, two decades later on *Natural Wonder* (and four decades later on the *Songs in the Key of Life* performance tour), the appeal is not encountering these aspects of the song as something new but feeling secure in knowing which ways the song goes and the slight chance that a live performance will allow you the chance to hear the song again for the first time. In other words, it's in the mix of nostalgia and in-the-moment experience captured in the song's lyrics, which looks back in the verses and embodies the potential ecstasy of music in its simple, one-line chorus: "You can feel it all over."

Despite hitting number one on the pop and R&B charts in 1977, "Sir Duke" has often been thought of as a poor relation to "I Wish," which equaled its chart positions. "Sir Duke" ends side one of the original vinyl album while "I Wish" gets preferential treatment leading off side two. Although they both dip into the same nostalgia well, "I Wish" is considered the deep sociological tract in which "nappy-headed boy" invokes centuries of Black oppression, whereas "Sir Duke" celebrates white jazz performer Glenn Miller. At times even Wonder seems to lean into this "Sir Duke" downgrade. At a 1981 Tokyo show with the two songs back-to-back, how they've typically been performed, "Sir Duke" is played first mostly as a throwaway audience participation number while "I Wish" follows as a serious performance, something that would happen repeatedly over the next forty years.

This is not to say that "Sir Duke" doesn't get its due on occasion. The May 4, 1985, performance at Motown Returns to the Apollo begins with a video salute and a few words about Sir Duke, Duke Ellington, and then launches into a respectful version that's admittedly a bit hollow without a live rhythm section.

Fortunately, on the 2014–2015 *Songs in the Key of Life* performance tour, Stevie let "Sir Duke" come to life on its own. Yes, it was still followed by "I Wish," but it was continually given aural space to expand and was played not as an obligation but as a pleasure, both recalling and embodying the joy of hearing the song for the first time. The performance of the song and the entire tour had no right being as good as they were.

Less than good is a performance of the song by singers Mac Davis, Donna Summer, and Harry Wayne Casey (KC of KC and the Sunshine Band) on Davis's May 11, 1978, NBC TV special *You Put Music in My Life*. Summer holds her own, but to call what Davis and KC are doing "singing" would be generous. If you find this online, make sure you have a safety word with an earplugged partner ready to hit pause just to be safe.

Chapter Eleven Playlist

"Everybody's Talkin'" (live), Stevie Wonder

"Ca' Purange," Dexter Gordon

"Ca' Purange" (live), Stevie Wonder

"Maria Elena," Los Indios Tabajaras

"Bridge over Troubled Water" (live), Stevie Wonder

"Shoo-Re-Doo-Be-Doo-Da-Day" (live), Stevie Wonder

"I'm Gonna Make You Love Me," Diana Ross and the Supremes
     and the Temptations

"For Once in My Life" (live), Stevie Wonder

"Stevie Ray Blues" (live), Stevie Wonder

"Stay Gold" (live), Stevie Wonder

"Gangsta's Paradise," Coolio featuring L.V.

SELECTED BIBLIOGRAPHY

This is not an exhaustive list, but these sources were most helpful in the writing of this book.

Askin, Noah, and Michael Mauskapf. "What Makes Popular Culture Popular? Product Features and Optimal Differentiation in Music." *American Sociological Review* 82 (October 1, 2017): 910–44.

Fleet, Paul, and Jonathon Winter. "Investigating the Origins of Contemporary Basics on the Drum Kit: An Exploration of the Role of the Hi-Hat in Anglo-American Popular Musics from 1960 until 1974." *Popular Music* 33, no. 2 (2014): 293–314.

Fulton, Will. "Reimagining the Collective: Black Popular Music and Recording Studio Innovation, 1970–1990" PhD diss., The Graduate Center, City University of New York, 2017. https://academicworks .cuny.edu/gc_etds/2012.

Hughes, Keith. *Don't Forget the Motor City: The Ultimate Guide to Motown (and Related Recordings) 1956–1972.* Last modified December 13, 2018. http://www.dftmc.info/index.html.

Hutchinson, Mick. *That Sounds Like Stevie! An Anthology of Wonder.* Billingham: Sixth Element Publishing, 2019.

Loder, Steve. *Stevie Wonder: A Musical Guide to the Classic Albums.* San Franciso: Backbeat, 2005.

Lundy, Zeth. *Songs in the Key of Life*. New York: Bloomsbury, 2007.

Perone, James E. *The Sound of Stevie Wonder: His Words and Music*. Westport, CT: Praeger Publishers, 2006.

Ribowsky, Mark. *Signed, Sealed, and Delivered: The Soulful Adventure of Stevie Wonder*. Hoboken, NJ: John Wiley & Sons, 2010.

Vincent, Rickey. *Funk: The Music, the People, and the Rhythm of the One*. New York: St. Martin's Griffin, 1996.

Werner, Craig. *Higher Ground: Stevie Wonder, Aretha Franklin, Curtis Mayfield, and the Rise and Fall of American Soul*. New York: Crown Publishers, 2004.